PRAISE FOR *BURYING HOME*

After knowing Todd for over 15 years, he still impresses me with his incredible ability to make you feel like you were part of the actual story. A story of what it means to be a true servant and a truly great man

REP. CHRIS WOOTEN

SOUTH CAROLINA HOUSE OF REPRESENTATIVES

Todd Carnes does a masterful job at describing how the grace of God not only overcomes an extremely dysfunctional family but also transforms three generations of family members. Unfiltered in expressing the pain he experienced along his journey, Todd highlights the power that the gospel has in changing lives, even the most hardened ones. Burying Home is a great story of God's love and forgiveness.

DR. BILL JONES, CHANCELLOR

COLUMBIA INTERNATIONAL UNIVERSITY

Burying Home hit home for me in so many ways. This is one book you will not be able to put down. I know God is good, but this book shows everyone that God is REAL good. It is amazing how His power can work in your heart and soul. So when you pick up this book, be ready to stand in awe of what can happen when you choose to believe!

KATHY MANESS

PRESIDENT, NATIONAL LEAGUE OF CITIES

EXEC. DIRECTOR, PALMETTO STATE TEACHERS ASSOCIATION

Burying Home is an amazing story about God's Grace and Salvation. I have known Todd for many years and he has been a trusted colleague and friend. This book hits home for me personally and professionally. Having also grown up in the south in the 1970s and having lost both my parents, this story is very familiar. I have also seen, lived and endured many of the "hidden or unspoken" transgressions in the story throughout my 25 year law enforcement career that are unfortunately still alive and well in today's world. Most of all, as many of you are fully aware, this book highlights that God always has a plan and that everything happens for a reason. I hope you enjoy this great story of a man's personal and spiritual journey through life as much as I did!

SHERIFF BRYAN "JAY" KOON

LEXINGTON COUNTY, SOUTH CAROLINA

Burying Home is a raw and inspiring true-life account of the ugliness and pain of abuse and addiction overcome by the grace and forgiveness found in the gospel of Jesus. As I read the initial chapters, at times I was tempted to despair at the tragedy of generations of men trapped in the claws of their vices. In the end, I found myself marveling at the power of the gospel to set men free from those vices and set a new trajectory for generations to come. Burying Home is a story worth your time.

DR. DOUG COLEMAN, PROFESSOR

CENTRAL ASIA

Burying Home is a thought provoking memoir that brings out into the open the kinds of dark secrets that overshadow many lives in our world today. It's transparency is engaging and a refreshing reminder that Jesus Christ still breaks the cycle of generational addictions. Through the twists and turns of the darkness, a minister was born who has touched the lives of many. God works in mysterious ways!

MICKEY LAYDEN, PRESIDENT/CEO
LCK CONSTRUCTION MANAGEMENT

BURYING HOME

MEMOIR OF A MILL VILLAGE MISSIONARY

BY
TODD CARNES

This book is typeset in EB Garamond

Paperback ISBN: 978-1-7359519-0-4
Ebook ISBN: 978-1-7359519-1-1

Designed by Hannah Gaskamp

Printed In The United States Of America
20 21 22 23 24 25 26 27 28 / 9 8 7 6 5 4 3 2 1

Dedicated to

Kerri, Laina, Amanda and Kristy,

Thanks for being patient with me as I have wrestled to take our family in a positive direction. The greatest feelings I have ever experienced were the four long hugs each of you provided for me on the day Chief died, the day I buried home. Your presence that day reminded me of how precious it is to be a part of our family.

And to Hunter Carnes

We walked this path together in the early days and I can't imagine how lonely I would feel if I didn't have you to reminisce with as I wrote this book about our childhood home.

This story is the accurate depiction of my memories, as verified by others with whom I have spoken. Some names have been changed to protect the privacy of others.

CONTENTS

PROLOGUE

I always knew I would write this book, but the thought of publishing it is unnerving. I knew I wanted to write these things down for my children and their children and beyond, but disclosing this story publicly brings with it real anxiety because it pulls the veil back and exposes long held family secrets. I have held these secrets deep in the recesses of my soul for forty-five-plus years, as has my brother, Hunter. These family secrets are painful and tragic, which is why I have generally felt as though the best course of action is to take them with me to the grave, never even divulging them in full to my own wife and children. Such secrecy is alluring to anyone who grew up in a home with troubling family secrets. That environment teaches us to feel an extraordinary amount of shame, even when we are not at fault. In fact, even as I began writing this account I felt like the ultimate traitor, the treasonous son who was exposing our family's shame. These feelings are the reason I would never entertain the thought of writing this memoir until this final season of life when only my brother and I are living.

Despite those fears, writing this story fulfills a great purpose. I love my family and have reconciled with my parents and where I came from; I do not intend to needlessly expose our darkest moments. I do, however, want to tell the story of my life with honesty and transparency. As a pastor for two decades, I often taught from my personal experience, yet I never fully pulled back the veil on my life. But my time in ministry taught me that many more families are struggling through difficult situations than we would naturally assume. This widespread experience, so often hidden in the shadows of our lives, compels me to write this story. We are all traveling this journey together, as strangers and pilgrims in this world, and I write this story for the benefit of my fellow travelers.

I am writing to the young man who feels extraordinary shame, not because of what he has done but because of the actions of others, so that he may be released.

I am writing to the young lady who has been raped by an evil man and feels as though she is somehow deserving of destructive relationships with men in her life, so that she might realize her worth and overcome this destructive lie.

I am writing to the family steeped in addiction for generations, that they might know how a single generation can free them.

I am writing to the single mother who labors long hours because she was abandoned by a selfish man, to remind her that her work will provide a better future for her children's children.

I am writing to the person who is the sole Christian in their family, to show them that while there is life, there is hope.

I am writing to the faithful believer who is about to give up on an old friend because of their continual drunkenness and bad decisions, in hopes they will hang on for one more year.

I am writing to the young man or woman who has an

audacious vision of what they might accomplish for God, so that they will hold to it fiercely when they are doubted.

I am writing to the young couple who is forced to mourn at their child's grave, to remind them of God's mercy in time of need.

I am writing to the child who has sufficient reason to remain angry with their parents forever, yet longs to find freedom in forgiving them.

Most importantly, I am writing to the person with their own story of pain and perseverance, but holds it in secret, convinced it is too shameful or insignificant to help others. I hope my story will bolster your courage and prod you to share your story to fellow travelers in this thing called life.

PART ONE:

MILL VILLAGE ROOTS

"We can ignore even pleasure. But pain insists upon being attended to. God whispers to us in our pleasures, speaks in our conscience, but shouts in our pains; it is His megaphone to rouse a deaf world.."

—C.S. Lewis, *The Problem of Pain*

INTRODUCTION

I t was Sunday as I walked into the small ranch home where I grew up. No one ever used the front door, for some reason, we just always used the garage entrance. As I opened the squeaky screen door on this day, I saw him lying in a hospice bed that had been installed in the living room in place of his trusted leather recliner. He was in a diaper with no other clothes, surrounded by Brenda and Janice. A week earlier he had been his normal self: sharp, witty, and brutally honest. But now it was different. In that small amount of time the lung cancer had taken over and his health had gone downhill tremendously. He was pitiful lying there in that bed, confused and disoriented.

As I walked in, I greeted him with the standard, "Hey Chief."

Surprisingly, he looked at Janice and asked, "Who is that?"

I couldn't believe my ears. "This is Todd," I said, incredulous that he didn't recognize me, his son. We were just talking last week during my visit about his home, his plans, his health. *And now he doesn't even know who I am?* It wasn't as upsetting as it was shocking. I never dreamed this would happen so quickly, though I was glad for the speed. My dad's future was going to be all pain and loneliness, things I didn't want for him and things he didn't want either, though he preferred them over death. Knowing the pain that was here and the pain coming, I was ready for him to pass from this life. And I knew about becoming a stranger in the eyes of a parent. My mother died with severe dementia when she was only sixty-two; she didn't know who I was for the last several years of her life as she languished in a nursing home. The last thing I wanted for Chief was for him to follow Mother's footsteps into the nursing home.

I settled onto the couch and began to talk to Brenda and Janice about all that was happening. This was an awkward conversation because both of these ladies were "dating" my father at the time and for the next several nights they both stayed at the house along with me. The house was a 1,400 sq. ft. ranch with only two bedrooms, so it was a rather tight squeeze for the four of us. It felt like even closer quarters with two ladies who were both dating the same man as we all watched him dying right in front of our eyes.

We managed to get through that Sunday night with regular doses of morphine and other high power, end-of-life prescription medicines. Then, late Monday afternoon, it happened. I was seated at the back of the den scrolling through my iPhone and he called out my name, "Todd, Todd, where are you? Todd, come here."

I was seated behind him so I don't know how in the world he knew I was there. Up until that time he either didn't know who I was or only acknowledged that I was there by calling me "that guy" or "that man." I got up and walked to his hospice bed, reaching for his hand through the rails.

CHAPTER 1

A FARMER PREACHER

My father went by many names in our family. His proper name was Homer Maise Carnes, but he was known as H. M. from his childhood. When I was about ten-years-old he once described to us how in every tribe there were many Indians, but there could only be one Chief. It was to be understood that in our house, he was the Chief. I have no idea what brought about this lesson in Native American hierarchy, but it somehow stuck, and from this point forward Daddy was primarily known as "Chief" by our family and most of my friends. Throughout this book I use the terms Daddy and Chief interchangeably, as I have throughout my life, but "Daddy" is the term of my childhood while "Chief" arrived in my teens.

Chief's grandfather was a man named John Carnes and, interestingly enough, he was a farmer preacher. At that time in

Alabama, they called these types of preachers "Hard Shell" Baptist preachers. Fundamentalist in their core beliefs, they also preached emotionally, an uncommon paring for sure. Once I went to a Hard Shell Baptist revival service with Daddy out in the country where his grandfather had lived. I have no idea why we went or even where we were. Several loud ministers were preaching at the time, moving up and down the aisles, wiping their mouths incessantly with a handkerchief as they shouted into microphones.

Then it happened. One older gentleman got caught up "in the Spirit." He went up front to testify and then came running to our aisle (there were only about eighty folks in the church). He looked at Chief and then literally crawled over me to get to him. The man got right up in Daddy's face and began to tell him that God had released him from all that whiskey they used to drink together. He said something about how he didn't even want that whiskey anymore and Daddy needed to get saved from his drinking, he needed God to deliver him from that evil whiskey. "H. M., you need to get free from that whiskey," he said. "I am saved and ain't never wanted another drop since the day I got saved. Never craved it again!"

Daddy was embarrassed. So was I. If we had been anywhere but church Daddy would have gotten fisty with the guy. Lucky for him we were at church, so Daddy just mumbled, "That is good Festus, glad to hear it, I am fine, don't worry about me." Neither of us mentioned the episode again; nor did we ever return to that place.

John Carnes, Chief's grandfather, preached at these type of churches – loud, boisterous, and chaotic. He raised his family, including my grandfather, in these kind of backwoods, peculiar churches. From what I've heard, John Carnes was a good man, though I never met him. He was a poor, hard-working farmer who cared for multiple kids. There was Rock, Morris, Malcolm, and Adele that I know of, though he may have had more kids I don't know about. Rock was famous for being a Golden Gloves champion boxer in his youth. For the first twenty years of my life, I never saw him sober. Rock would often come to our house after a long day of work as a carpenter or roofer and drink with Daddy. At times he would try to teach me to box in the back of our den. I always wished that he could actually be sober and teach me to fight. I sincerely wanted to learn since I often got picked on as the youngest in our neighborhood. Unfortunately, those lessons never happened. Rock was every bit as intimidating as his name sounds. I remember asking Daddy about his real street fighting ability when I got a little older. He confirmed that Rock would hurt you out on the street.

I never met Malcolm, but by all accounts he was a good man, the son who took after his father and embraced the faith throughout his life. Adele was raised in the same environment and became pretty tough along the way. She was infamous for shooting her husband—multiple times! The legend was that she shot him at least twice, both times in the leg, for running around with other ladies. Each time she found out that he was sleeping with someone else, she shot him. What is more astounding is that he was a police officer. That meant every time he was shot by his wife, it was reported that he accidentally shot himself while cleaning his firearm. If she had only aimed a little higher she could have put a full stop to that running around! Those were good days when life was just that simple: you cheat on your wife and she shoots you in the leg as a warning. Repeat as needed!

Then there was Morris, Chief's father. Chief despised him. I only met him once in my life. My brother, Hunter, and I were out in our backyard on our swing set and Daddy was out there with us, which was highly unusual for him. Morris suddenly appeared and I had no idea who he was. He was driving a convertible, something we had never seen before. After Chief introduced him awkwardly, he gave us a ride around the block in his convertible and then handed us each a brand-new silver dollar that was inside of an orange plastic piggy bank from Panama City Beach, Florida. It was the only time I ever saw him. Soon after that he died and I was too young to go to the funeral. I suppose he knew he had cancer when he came by, which was the reason for the trip, but I am not sure. My brother attended the funeral and said he saw Chief crying in a way he had never seen before. Daddy wasn't close to Morris and was even hostile toward him, but at the end of the day your daddy is your daddy and nothing can ever change that. Even if he is sorry at times, or sorry most of the time, as was the case with Morris, you are forever linked to him and have a deep connection. Your relationship with your father is one of the most powerful relationships within every human heart, and it has a ripple effect throughout life.

According to legend, Morris was a real piece of work. He fathered two children with his wife, Zana, and then left her for another woman, Ruth. At that time both Zana and Morris worked in the Dwight Manufacturing Company cotton mill, one of the largest cotton mills in the South. According to Chief, from the day Morris abandoned his family, he spent all of his time and energy trying to not pay child support. Chief said his only real memories of Morris were when they were in court trying to get him to pay his child support and he was trying to weasel out of it. Zana was feisty, though, and somehow managed to get Morris drafted into the army in his late twenties so that his wages could be garnished and she could get some help raising these two children with more than her single income as a cotton mill laborer. I don't know how long he was in the armed services, but he was discharged after several years and went about living his life apart from his children with his new bride, never providing any financial help to Zana or his children. It is a terrible legacy.

And so Daddy grew up in the mill village on Sandusky Lane, living with his sister, Juanita, his mother, Zana, and both of Zana's parents. According to Chief, they were all desperately poor, but so was everyone else; and he had a great time as a child with the other children in the village. They washed their feet in the sink every night and took a bath once a week. They ate beans and vegetables all through the week and had meat when they butchered a chicken on Saturdays. They had no heat other than a coal burning fireplace that went out at night and had to be stoked early in the morning to bring relief from the frost. Yet they had fun, spending most of their time outside, playing with other children, barefoot and shirtless whenever possible. Their toy of choice was called a "caso," which was an old, used car tire they rolled around the dirt roads. They had games and fights on a regular basis, but for the most part shared a real sense of community, with all the adults looking out for all the children.

Daddy's stories reminded me of just how much times have changed. This was before Jonas Salk's polio vaccine, so every summer in the mill village it was a given that a couple of people, usually children, were going to be stricken with polio. When this happened, the health department would come out and tape off their house to quarantine the entire family until the disease had passed. It was a brutal time for all families as it felt like Russian roulette every summer with your children's health.

He also described for me how they used to walk six miles one way just to go skating at night, then six miles back home because if they didn't waste a nickel on the bus ride, they could buy a Coca-Cola, a rare pleasure. Perhaps one of the stranger things was that his grandmother was some type of natural medicine woman. Once he had warts on his foot, and she gave him a nickel and told him that she had bought these warts from him and they would disappear as long as he didn't spend the nickel. He hid it under a rug and soon the warts were gone. She also was known far and wide as the person who could heal thrush in infants, which was a very serious condition before baby formula was invented. Moms would bring oak leaves to their house and his grandmother would take them into a back room and perform some type of procedure or séance, I am not sure which. Regardless, he said it always worked. The most bothersome part is that she told Daddy she could only tell her medicinal secrets to a person who had never seen her real father, which strikes me as rather occult-like, even though Daddy always said she was a very religious person.

When he was about thirteen, Daddy took on his first job as a paper boy. He got a route in the mill village and started throwing papers every morning before the sun came up. Being a paper boy at that time was no easy task. It meant rising every day, seven days a week, at about four or five a.m., riding your bicycle three or four miles to the *Gadsden Times* office, picking up several hundred unfolded papers, and taking them home to fold so they could be thrown onto porches. Once folded, you would put them into your bag and hit your route, where you had memorized which houses received the paper and which did not. As you rode your route, you would then throw the paper onto their porches with precise aim. This happened rain or shine, as there was no backup plan to get the papers out. Daddy told me the supervisor at the *Gadsden Times* would threaten to physically whip these paper boys with a belt if they missed a day or otherwise messed up their route.

After doing this for some time, he was able to upgrade from his bicycle to a motorcycle. This motorcycle would change his life. One day he was out joy riding and had an accident where his left foot was caught in the fender well of a car that had backed out in front of him. It crushed his foot and broke a lot of bones in his ankle. It was the early 1950s and medical care was still rather primitive by today's standards, so he was immediately shipped off to the Children's Hospital in Birmingham for treatment, sixty miles from the Dwight mill village. They had to do multiple skin grafts to attempt a full rebuild of his broken and mangled foot.

The accident caused him to miss an entire year of school, so to keep himself busy he found a guy who could teach him how to play the drums. He became a very accomplished drummer, eventually playing drums at the University of Alabama and in some small bands for local clubs. (He kept University of Alabama drumming medals prominently displayed in our home, awarded for his abilities as a lead drummer. He thought so much of these medals we actually buried them with him!) He was always industrious and quite the salesman. He eventually parlayed his knowledge of drumming into learning how to drive, convincing a guy to teach him in exchange for drum lessons. It is obvious who got the better end of that deal!

Daddy went on to finish high school, and because he had a disability, he received some grant money to go to the University of Alabama. This was a first, as most folks from the mill village barely made it out of high school. He didn't have a car so he often hitchhiked from Gadsden to Tuscaloosa on the weekends, about a three-hour drive at the time. He said all he had to do was put a big Alabama sticker on his suitcase and folks would know he was a university student and gladly give him a ride. I think he had a great time at college. He played drums, pledged Sigma Phi Epsilon fraternity, and seemingly performed well for several years. Much like would happen with me years later, however, it was during this season of his life when addiction to alcohol took root and began to destroy him. He was smart enough that he could have finished any major at the University of Alabama, but after three years he was more devoted to partying than to education. Also, as a born entrepreneur, he was ready to get out into the world and make some money.

His brother-in-law, Bill McCollum, was out making money as a door-to-door fiberglass attic insulation salesman, and eventually his continuous invitations were too much to resist. Daddy quit school and went to work alongside Bill because he wanted to buy a fancy car. He always said that for the next twenty years he would tell himself that he was going back to school to finish his degree "next year." Finally, he admitted to himself that he was never going back. Indeed, he couldn't return to finish his degree with three other mouths to feed. He regretted a lot of things in life, and not finishing college was near the top of that list. I think only later did he realize just how smart he was and how easy it would have been to finish a challenging degree, like physics or engineering. At the time, however, he just couldn't comprehend the relevance of it all. That is why he pushed me so hard to go to school and get my degree, which I did; and I became the first person in our family to earn a college degree.

His tactics for driving this point about education home were very effective during my teen years. He was by then a home remodeling contractor, and my brother and I worked for him every summer. It was a great job that paid us $5 an hour, and that was a lot of money in the 1980s. Many days he would take me out to a new room addition job he had sold and he would put up batter boards and shoot floor elevations to "lay out" the room with string. That was the white-collar work on the site. After that, he would throw out a pickax, a round and flat shovel, and some cloth gloves, while instructing me that he needed a foundation twenty-four inches wide and eight inches deep across the entire exterior of the new room, often fifty or more linear feet. Then he would drive off. Sometimes I would do this together with my brother, sometimes alone. Most of these jobs were in the Black section of town[1]. Ever the entrepreneur, Daddy had found a way to get FHA loans for low income households so they could add a room or two to their small homes. So there I was, a skinny white kid in the Black section of our segregated town, digging in a backyard all day long hoping trouble didn't find me.

Daddy would often come by around lunchtime and bring me something to eat and a Coke. There was a glorious barbecue place there called Penny Profit that had massive sandwiches I will never forget. They were tangy with just enough spice to make your mouth water. At some point during lunch, he would say, "Son, if you don't want to dig ditches all your life, you will go to school and get yourself a civil engineering degree. Then you can ride around in the air-conditioned truck instead of sweating like a borrowed mule out here."

If I heard it once, I heard it a hundred times, and it worked

1 The terminology of white and black may sound offensive to some today, but at this time it was the common terminology throughout America. Also, Gadsden was almost 100 percent segregated by neighborhood, as public schools were not integrated until the early 1970's.

even though I didn't even know what an engineer was until my junior year at the University of Alabama. I thought it was construction management, not design work, and probably couldn't distinguish between the two. But I trusted what he said and studied civil engineering and finished that degree, which has served me well all my life. He did right in that regard, as every father wants his kids to overcome his own crucial mistakes in life. He was so proud of the fact that I received that degree, and I pursued it in large part because of those ninety-five-degree days digging ditches in an unfamiliar and unnerving section of town for a white kid in the segregated South.

Chief in the mill village

Chief's grandmother - The village medicine woman

CHAPTER 2

A RURAL TRIBE

As colorful as Chief's family was and is, my mother's family was even more so. Her parents were Ed and Gladys White of Hollypond, Alabama, a very small, rural community of farmers. It is one of those charming little towns where life is difficult yet simple. Poverty was not the exception, but the rule. Doctors and dentists were rare, and even more rarely utilized. Most everyone farmed and raised some type of livestock to make ends meet. Dirt roads were more common than paved and the only source of air-conditioning was box fans or sitting under the shade tree.

As is generally the case, in these types of poor communities where everyone works hard, there is an honor code that demands that you honor another man's work. This means you can't steal from him because he worked hard to produce whatever he has. This code does not exist in most urban environments, but clearly it did in Hollypond. There are two stories that illustrate this very well. As a child, I often went to the very small grocery store with

Gladys (we called her Mama White), and at the checkout line she would hand her checkbook over to the cashier. Mama White could not write out a check herself because she was not able to go to school as a child, so she had to trust the cashier to do it for her and not take advantage of her. After the check was filled out, Mama White would sign it. Years later my wife, Kerri, and I were passing through and stopped at a fruit stand on the side of a major two-lane road. The prices were marked on pieces of cardboard since the owners were not at the stand at that time. You were instructed to take the fruit you wanted and then put your money in a box. The box had a slit in the top and was closed with a lock, but nothing prevented someone from either not paying or taking the entire box of money. Can you imagine that happening in any urban environment?

Ed White had at least five siblings and Gladys had at least three (in both cases there may have been others I never met or knew). Gladys's side of the family was not well-known to me other than a brother, Hubert, who was married to Lovie and lived on Papa Ed's land. Hubert was a mystery to me. I hardly remember him ever speaking although I was around him a decent amount as a child. He was old and frail, sitting in a chair in his house wearing his denim overalls (everyone there wore overalls, no exceptions), smoking hand-rolled Prince Albert cigarettes. His house was tiny, positioned at the back of Papa Ed's land.

His life was interesting, though. The story I always heard was that Hubert was caught bootlegging moonshine as a young man and was told he was either going to go to the front lines of the war as an infantry solider or to prison. He chose the front lines, where he was involved in lots of very close combat battles. Chief said that once, when Hubert was drunk late at night, he told him about a German soldier sneaking up stealthily and jumping out to surprise him with rifle drawn. The German then pulled the trigger to his rifle at twenty feet or less, and the weapon inexplicably jammed. Hubert was then able to draw his weapon and kill the man at point-blank range. He said he could never forget seeing the absolute terror in the young German's eyes when his weapon jammed and he knew he was going to die. Chief said Hubert never discussed these things except late at night when he was really drunk, so I am sure these experiences wounded Hubert in a way that no one knew how to deal with in the 1940s and '50s. Thus, he sat at home and drank heavily to cope with what we now know as PTSD.

On the brighter side, my grandmother had one relative, whose name I don't remember, who was a country preacher and who had a lot of children, five or more as I recall. He was famous among my grandmother's family for being so humble that he and his wife would put out dinner for his family each night and he would wait until everyone else had eaten before taking a bite. After everyone else had eaten, he would go behind his children and eat anything that they'd left on their plates, because they were too poor to afford enough food. His kids went on to be very successful across the country and his legacy stretched out far and wide for his faith and humility. Everyone spoke so highly of him at every family reunion. These are the kinds of people I think of when I recall the Biblical promise that "the first will be last and the last will be first."

Papa Ed's family, on the other hand, was a crazy cast of characters. His brother, Argyle, lived next door (which means about two hundred yards away in the country) with his wife, Novie, and worked in factories while raising hogs, chickens, and two boys,

Jimmy and Danny. There are too many Argyle stories to recount, but the one that encapsulates him the most is related to his relationship with his bulldog, Peanut. He had trained Peanut to guard the house and attack a pig or sow at his command. Occasionally Peanut would not immediately comply with Argyle's demands and the one thing that Argyle could not tolerate was anyone in his house not obeying him instantly. Not once but several times, Argyle loaded his shotgun with birdshot and chased Peanut off about forty yards so he could shoot him for not obeying. Whenever Argyle did this, Peanut would run the two hundred or so yards to Papa Ed's house all bloody, crawl under the house, and stay there for a day or two healing up before going back to his master. It was a hard life for Peanut and for others, as Argyle was a tough nut. He served in the navy during the war but I never heard any war stories from him, only talk about being on the really large ships and going to Japan.

Argyle's wife, Novie, didn't have an easy road either, as Argyle could be really harsh and demanding. Novie was known for her hard work and hard jobs. She cleaned homes for locals and local chicken houses as well. When I used to hear about her cleaning chicken houses, I always wondered what that meant but was afraid to ask. I though perhaps she was washing windows and walls in those massive chicken houses that seemed to be everywhere in Hollypond? In reality, cleaning chicken houses means walking through and cleaning up chicken droppings and pulling out dead chickens, etc. She was also expected to maintain Argyle's home and cook for everyone, as people in Hollypond rarely went out to eat at this time. First of all, there were no restaurants nearby. Second, these folks had grown up eating at home so dining at a restaurant was not something they ever wanted or needed. At home, the staples were milk and bread (hand-crushed cornbread in a glass with whole milk poured over it and eaten with a spoon), fried eggs from the laying hens, and whatever fruit was in season, as there were lots of fruit trees and berry bushes around. For meat, there was always plenty of pork since they would kill a hog every season and put up the meat for the coming year.

Jack was Papa Ed's other brother, and legend has it that Jack White was the meanest man to ever come out of Cullman County. Chief told me stories of Jack shooting guys with a .22-caliber rifle, running out of bullets, and using the butt of the rifle to beat them after he shot them. Hollypond was the Wild West back in the early 1900s and law enforcement was few and far between, so incidents like this really happened. Jack was feared throughout the entire county, even when he was in his sixties.

One time when Jack and Papa Ed got drunk and played cards, and they were gambling hard-earned money, something happened along the way and Jack stabbed Papa Ed. He just barely missed Papa Ed's heart but managed to collapse his lung. Somehow Papa Ed survived and they actually reconciled pretty quickly. There are various accounts about why Jack stabbed his brother that night. Some say Ed had a gun, others say Jack lost his money and did what Jack does. No one really knows and I don't know that either of them ever divulged exactly what happened—they were probably so drunk they didn't even remember!

When I was a very young boy, almost every evening Jack would walk from his trailer to Papa Ed's house, which was about a quarter mile away straight down the dirt road on family land. He would come in to sit and watch television with Papa Ed since he didn't have a television of his own. If it was cold, Papa Ed would ask if he wanted to stay the night, and he never would, returning to his house around eleven p.m. after the local news or *Hee Haw* or *Gunsmoke*—whatever we were watching that night. Jack rarely spoke and was never shaved, but when he did speak he had a really deep, John Wayne–type voice. I have only recently discovered that he had several children, but I only knew one, his son Roger.

Roger lived with Jack in that very small trailer, which I think was really just a camper. I never went inside of it even though I passed it often. I can only imagine how sparse it was and who knows how and when they ate. I think Jack's sister, Willie Bell, fed them most of the time since she lived next door. But Roger was definitely a modern-day Huck Finn. He never wore shoes, rarely went to school, was mischievous in all things and tough as nails. I will never forget watching him sprint barefoot down the old gravel road in front of Papa Ed's house—I was amazed that he could do that, as I could barely walk on that gravel with shoes! Roger eventually left Hollypond and went to work with "some big outfit catching chickens." At the time I didn't even know what that meant, but later learned he was hired to literally catch chickens and load them up for processing. I don't know whatever happened to Roger; folks would ask from time to time if anyone had heard from him and it seemed that he would go years without any contact back home. I have no idea what life really looked like for him, but knowing Jack's reputation I imagine it was incredibly tough.

There was another brother, Shorty, who was the baby of the bunch. He actually got out of Hollypond and moved to Birmingham and maybe even finished college at some point. Then there were the sisters, Willie Bell and Vida. They both lived in the area and raised their families there, though Vida made a sojourn to California at some point. Willie Bell always stood out because she chewed Red Man tobacco instead of dipping Tops Sweet Snuff like everyone else. As far as I know, every adult either dipped, chewed, or smoked, and most did all three. This obviously had a disastrous effect on their teeth, and most of them didn't have any real teeth at all, only full sets of dentures. I am sure some slick dentist convinced them to have all their teeth pulled at some point and sold them dentures, which were often inside a glass cup in the kitchen, ironically having been taken out to eat.

I didn't really know Vida and thought her name was "Vider" up until recently, as that is how it was always pronounced. In Hollypond, an *r* sound was added to almost any word where it would fit, such as *yeller, feller, bananer, fur* instead of *for*, etc. Willie Bell was always warm and inviting and had the most memorable laugh. My favorite story about her is how they hosted the viewing in her house when her husband, Cobb, died. At that time, it was somewhat common to keep the body in the house for folks to come and view before the burial. When Cobb died they kept him in the house for a day or so. Country folks are somewhat superstitious and these houses are only about a thousand square feet. That means everyone is very near the body at all times, so someone had to stay up "with the body" all night. Daddy told me he and Mother and others volunteered to stay up. I barely remember seeing Cobb in that little room, but I do remember all the local people coming out to pay their respects. Country folk have pride and honor and always showed the appropriate respect in times such as these.

My grandparent's home in Hollypond was the land of safety for me as a child. I recently told my wife that every now and then I have a dream where I am waking up early at Mama White's house and she is cooking. I am sleeping by the open screened-in door to beat the heat in the house cooled only with fans. I can smell the tenderloin and biscuits as I roll over in the bed. When I have this dream I am always depressed when I wake up, because it is the one dream where I just want to stay there in that place of love and acceptance and peace. Mama White and Papa Ed were a hiding place during my childhood. Papa Ed would play cards with me all night and take me out to the hog feeder in the woods during the day. He bought me a pet goat (named Billy, of course), a go-cart, and a million Mountain Dews. Mama White cooked for us all the time, peeling our peaches, baking us cakes, and giving us everything she had. She also took me to her Rook card nights, where she played with three other ladies. They would always let me deal the cards for them. I vividly remember her cooking pork tenderloin pieces many mornings and letting me eat the very small pieces of meat. She would then come behind me and eat the fat meat I had peeled away from the good meat. Looking back, that was probably out of necessity.

Mama White and Papa Ed worked hard all their lives and had almost nothing materially to show for it, but they were the best grandparents the world has ever seen. They had to know the hell we were enduring in our house, so they always made room for us at their home. During these years, until I was about twelve-years-old, their house was like heaven to me. Papa Ed drank quite a bit when he was working in the mill and raising Mother, but he was golden as a grandfather. When I asked why or how he stopped drinking, I was told that he simply stated that he didn't ever want his grandkids to see him drunk, so he quit cold turkey when my older brother was adopted into the family.

There is one story that has to be told in contradiction to the above, as I only saw Papa Ed drink one time in my life. One evening when I was about ten years old, Papa Ed and Chief were going to a cock fight out in the country and somehow I managed to convince them to take me along. When we arrived there seemed to be a hundred or more people there, waiting to get inside the barn and gamble on the cocks. While we were waiting Chief was playing some dice game on the tailgate of his truck and gambling with whoever wanted to play. Both he and Papa Ed were drinking and getting drunker by the minute. I wanted so badly to go inside and see a real cock fight, as I was told the roosters would fight to the death. At some point in the night, while Chief was still gambling on the tailgate, the local Sheriff showed up and put the two organizers in handcuffs and told everyone else they better "get the hell outta here!" That word somehow got to us on the outside so we loaded up quickly and hit the road. By the time we arrived back home, well after midnight, Papa Ed and Daddy were both sloppy drunk. As we were walking up to the house, Mama White came out of the front door yelling and cursing at Papa Ed for having me out with them while they were drinking like that. I really thought she was going to hit him. He didn't say a word in reply, probably because he knew how wrong he was to have me with them. At the time, I thought it was the coolest thing to have gone and was only upset I didn't get to see the cocks fight. After this, me and Papa Ed would make muscadine wine together from fresh muscadines and sell it in gallon milk jugs, often after it had aged 5+ years and presumably become muscadine whiskey, but I never saw him drink again.

Mama White & Papa Ed

My safe house as a child (also pictured on book cover)

CHAPTER 3

MILL VILLAGE MATRIMONY

These two mill village families, the Carnes and the Whites, were the cast of characters that formed the background of my Carnes family, which lived for fifty years at 3704 Roselawn Drive in Alabama City, Alabama (later known as Gadsden). On the one side you have H. M. Carnes, the young man who grew up determined and self-reliant after his dad walked out on the family. On the other, you have Shirley White, my mother, who grew up as the only child of a rural farming couple who were drawn to the mill village by the promise of steady work at the Dwight Industries cotton mill. She received a high school education, something her parents greatly valued since they were only able to complete the third or fourth grade before being called into the fields to work. Mama White often told me the story of how she escaped those same fields when she was taken out of school in third grade. She hated hoeing weeds so much that she begged to come inside to cook instead. At that time she was too short to reach the top of the oven. This didn't deter her, though. She just put a five-gallon bucket in front of the stove to stand on and, at age nine or so, started to cook for the others who were out working the fields. After sixty years of practice, she was awesome at cooking home-made biscuits, jams, cornbread, tenderloin, vegetable soup, cakes of all kinds—you name it!

Growing up in the mill village, Shirley and H.M. both attended Dwight Industries primary schools and then went to Emma Sansom High School. Emma Sansom was a local Civil War hero-ine who has a prominent statue in Gadsden to this day. Her claim to fame is that she showed General Nathan Bedford Forrest a shal-low spot where he and his men could cross Black Creek when they were pursuing Union Colonel Abel Streight, who had burned the bridge after traversing it with his men. Later, a middle school would be named for General Forrest and he would get a very prominent statue as well. The most ironic thing about all of this is that these two schools were situated adjacent to a large public housing com-plex of hundreds of units that were exclusively African American. Looking back, I never heard a single person complain or even bring up the stark irony of this scenario, which is not that uncommon in the South. To be frank, not until I had been away from Gadsden for a decade or more did I even recognize the irony of it myself. When you grew up there, it somehow seemed normal.

Shirley and H.M. knew each other in middle school and dated some in high school. H.M. entered the University of Alabama a year or two before Shirley graduated high school. Then Shirley went to Gadsden Business School and learned administra-tive skills, like typing and shorthand. As noted earlier, H.M. left college after three years and hit the road as a traveling salesman with Bill McCollum in order to buy that new car he wanted. Short-term gain, long-term pain! That is the constant trap of youth, and Daddy always lamented it by saying, "Youth is wasted on the young."

Chief and Bill traveled all over selling insulation door to door, from Mississippi to Texas to Georgia and back. Chief's favorite story about that time was how one night he and Bill were making a house call trying to get a sale they desperately needed for their quota. They took a man and his wife all the way through the pitch book of pictures and information and asked them to sign up and purchase. The gentleman was warm to the idea but not ready to move forward. When he declined, Bill didn't hesitate. He flipped the pitch book all the way back to the front page and plainly said, "If you are not ready to buy this product, I must not have explained it clearly enough, so we need to run through it again." It was already late in the evening and they were wearing the gentleman down. When they finished going through the entire pitch a second time, the gentleman signed the contract. It was in this rough-and-tumble door-to-door environment that Daddy learned to sell. Later in life, he could truly sell ice to an Eskimo.

After several years, Chief used his intellect and natural ambition to figure out just how much the insulation cost, how much it was to install, and what price they were charging customers. Armed with this knowledge and the determination he had developed as a thirteen-year-old paper boy, he came up with the money to buy an insulation blowing truck of his own and started doing his own sales and operations. I asked him how he survived, and he said that some of the guys with his former company would make sales and do them "off the official paper" and give those sales to him, for a generous cash commission. During these early days Chief hustled, and often got hustled I am sure, but he was learning how business works and how to succeed. He would take these early lessons and build on them as he went from selling insulation to selling awnings to selling whatever a customer might want for their house. His determination is what allowed me to take another step forward in life and earn a college degree.

At some point while Daddy was working with Bill, Shirley White went down to Greenville, Mississippi, where Daddy was living. They were married by a justice of the peace. As a child, I never heard a word about their marriage. At the end of his life Daddy told me that Mother came down there specifically to get him to marry her. He was ashamed to tell me that and didn't even say it very clearly, just hinted at it enough so that I knew what he was saying. Looking back, I am sure that was the case, though it was a tragic choice for her. Since it was such a taboo subject, I wonder what the circumstances might have been. Was Mother pregnant and subsequently lost the child? Or maybe she just thought she was pregnant?

Unfortunately, I will never know how and why it happened this way, but I do know that at that time in our family it was common for folks to simply get married in a house. I remember one of my cousins getting married in the living room of our very small home. I think Bill and Juanita were married in Mama Zana's home. I would be willing to bet that none of my grandparents had an actual church wedding as we think of them today, but rather signed papers or even signed in a Bible insert with a justice of the peace. I might have been the first person in my family to have a wedding ceremony in a church.

They didn't live for long in Greenville, Mississippi before they moved back home to Gadsden. I can't imagine how they'd been living in Greenville. At the time Daddy was a hard partier and Mother was always a follower so she did whatever Daddy expected of her. That meant she was partying as well. When Daddy came home, he continued selling insulation and very quickly began selling awnings as well, as that was the hot new thing. In those days he would put on a suit and go sell door to door all day, only to return home that night to put on old clothes and build whatever he had sold. The next day he would go and do the installation. It was hard work, but Daddy was always very industrious and confident in his abilities, so he could make it happen regardless of the obstacles. Those few times when he couldn't, he would run to the whiskey bottle and self-medicate for a few days before getting back into the flow of life. From these beginnings in insulation and awnings, he continued to add a few products here and there and eventually formed Carnes Construction Company, which he ran primarily out of our den all my life. He would take on any and all types of remodeling projects for fifty years to provide for his family, for which I am eternally grateful. He didn't have any advantage given to him in life, yet he single-handedly lifted our family out of the poverty of the mill village and gave us opportunities he could have never imagined as a child.

As is often the case, I never really grasped what a herculean feat this was for him until I was in my thirties. At that time, when I had the responsibility of five mouths to feed and futures to secure, I was able to reflect on Chief's life and how he had totally revamped the financial futures of our family with his ingenuity and hustle. I wrote him several letters about this during those years, honoring him as my father and thanking him over and over for everything he sacrificed. Poverty is a killer of dreams and ambition, so to overcome it for your family is indeed a noble and honorable task worthy of praise.

Mother and Daddy with Hunter

Mother and Daddy with Mama White and Papa Ed

CHAPTER 4

MY FATHER'S HOUSE

H.M. and Shirley landed in a house on Hoke Street in East Gadsden around 1965 when they first returned to the area. I remember Chief telling me they had to write home and ask for gas money to get home from Mississippi. Daddy had to drive that big ole insulation-blower truck back to Gadsden for a new start. At that time, they had a neighbor named Danny Ford, who went on to become a very famous college football coach at multiple schools and won a national championship at Clemson University. Chief often talked about seeing Danny out mowing his lawn in those days and just how thick and strong a young man he was. In 1967 or 1968, H.M. and Shirley bought our home at 3704 Roselawn Drive. I am pretty sure it was a dump when they bought it because Mother cried the first time she saw it. Daddy, however, was the consummate optimist. He went to work fixing it up and made this three-bedroom, two-bath, fourteen-hundred-square-foot ranch house a comfortable home for our family for the next half century. It will always be my home.

After being married for a number of years and not having children, H.M. and Shirley became anxious and worried they would never conceive. I don't know if they had input from doctors about this or just came to their own conclusions, but either way they started down the path of adoption. I can imagine at that time my mother was often alone at home and wanted some children that could absorb all the excess love she had in her heart. In the 1960s, adoption was only facilitated via the state government and there was a very well-defined process for vetting a couple prior to allowing them to adopt. Included in this process were surprise visits by social workers. The reality of that was nerve-wracking for Mother because she never knew when Daddy was going to be drunk or sober and she was terrified that they would get a visit when he was home drunk and their hopes of adoption would be terminated. By the grace of God, this never happened and they were able to make it through the vetting process and were placed on the list to adopt.

I have no idea how long it took, but eventually they were called to Montgomery, the state capital, to pick up their child. They were placed in an empty room where they had to sit and wait for what seemed like forever with no communication at all. Finally, a social worker walked in and placed a little boy into their arms and they became parents. The child was about six months old and his name was Michael Anthony Godwin. He was from Selma, Alabama.

The story Chief told me was that the state officials told them the mom was a very young girl, fifteen or so, and the father was not willing to be involved. He said they gave him a profile of the dad and that he was supposedly a man of about 5'5", which Daddy always mocked because Michael Anthony Godwin (whom they subsequently named Hunter Michael Carnes) turned out to be 6'7"!

Hunter came with a stuffed animal named Bama that was precious to him throughout his childhood. I remember that very well because if I ever really got mad at him, I would get Bama and throw him or pull some of his fur out. He should have buried me for that, but I always escaped! Mother also told me that Hunter had a deformed head when they got him because he had spent so much time lying in a crib in a foster home. If a child lies only on one side and isn't turned periodically, their very malleable skull will flatten out on one side. This actually happened to one of my daughters, so it is not necessarily a sign of neglect by the foster parents. Regardless, once they had their new son they had to spend significant time trying to rectify that issue while he was young, and they were successful, as was I with my own daughter. They loved their new son dearly and were very proud parents.

Just over a year after welcoming Hunter into their home, they found out they were pregnant with me. I can only imagine the surprise and joy, as they never thought they would have even one son and now they were going to have two! I was born at St. James Catholic hospital, with the help of nuns attending to Mother as she labored through delivery. She often told me that story and I would try to imagine nuns with big habits on either side of a hospital bed coaching my frail mother along during labor and delivery. It seems that I didn't necessarily want to come out and my mother was very small, so the doctor eventually had to grab me by the head with forceps and pull me out, which resulted in me having what Daddy always called a "black eye" at birth. I remember Daddy telling this story to others throughout my childhood saying, "There I was, looking into the nursery from the hallway and the nurse picks up this baby with a big-ass shiner on his eye, and I was thinking there's no way that ugly little son of a bitch is mine, but she just nodded through the glass and it was you, black eye and all!" At that time, that was just how he talked and I didn't take it in any way other than a funny story.

I was named Anthony Todd Carnes, taking Anthony from my brother's birth name, a fact I never learned until I was over forty years old. I had always wondered where my first name originated and even asked my parents about it several times. Each time I was always dismissed with some mumblings that didn't make sense and never received a straight answer. It was another family secret. Even so, this is the story of how this second generation Carnes family was created in the house located at 3704 Roselawn Drive in Alabama City, Alabama.

Following our births, I am not sure if there was any honeymoon period with Mother and Daddy or if the chaos that I witnessed throughout my life was already a reality of our home at that time. The only thing I can speak of authoritatively is my first memories in this house on Roselawn Drive. There were both good and bad. I remember playing countless hours of football, basketball, and Wiffle Ball all over our neighborhood. We had a slew of boys around, and one really athletic girl, Kelly Gross, whose father coached the high school football team. In our neighborhood, we would play outside from mid-morning through late evening. We often played basketball till we couldn't see, as we only had one misaligned flood light for lighting at night. When it became too dark, we would transition to catching lightning bugs, running through the toxic fogger truck that rode the streets spraying for mosquitoes, and playing hide-and-seek. I still vividly remember when Daddy came home with a large metal post to assemble our very own basketball hoop . . . one of the best memories I have for sure. That basketball hoop was great for years, until my 6'10" neighbor, "Big Todd," as opposed to me, "Little Todd," came over and dunked on it à la Michael Jordan, destroying it. Chief was so furious he went straight over to Big Todd's house and took the brand-new hoop out of their garage to replace ours.

That wasn't the only time Big Todd got us into trouble. As the oldest in the neighborhood, he was the alpha who could get us all to do just about anything. There was the time he stole a bunch of flares from the railroad tracks that ran right beside our neighborhood. This wasn't one set of tracks, mind you, it was a full transfer station. (These are the same tracks from which a hobo crossed through one of our backyard football games and scared us all to death. He had on the overalls and was carrying his clothes on a bandanna wrapped around a stick, just as you might have seen on a television show at the time.) With the flares, we lit a few, held them for a few seconds, then threw them into the woods. Guess how that turned out? Yep, woods on fire next to Mr. Ratliff's house, with four excited boys trying to put it out with two one-gallon buckets hauled from a hundred yards away. That led to a long lecture by the local firemen, who were called by someone's parents and came to put out the fire. That led to a long lecture back at the house.

Big Todd also convinced us all to break into a neighborhood house. Well, we didn't really break in because the door was left open, but we went in and milled around, looking for something to steal. As I remember, the only thing we found was a tin box of Sucrets throat lozenges. Somehow, we all got caught and I distinctly remember Chief putting me and Hunter on the couch and threatening to call the police on us and then talking about sending us off to a military school if we were going to keep doing things like this. I have no idea if he was serious about either of these threats, but I know Mother would have never allowed this to happen. The threats, however, worked.

Beyond these sports and games, there were plenty of fights with many boys in the neighborhood. The one I remember best was when someone came up with a set of boxing gloves—one set of only two gloves. For us to use them, we could only use one hand each, the person with the left-handed glove at a clear disadvantage. Hunter took on Sam Harper in our backyard with only one hand to throw haymakers at each other. It didn't last long, as fighting with only one hand didn't work out well after all.

Those were the tame fights. The more common were the bare-knuckle ones. There was that time my brother and Trey, Big Todd's younger brother, got into a fight and I tried to help, only to be thrown into the bushes by Big Todd. When I recounted this to Big Todd's dad, Jerry, he told me to pick something up and knock Big Todd in the head with it if he tried to do that again. Yea, he was talking about his own son—it was a tough neighborhood.

The best fights, however, were always between brothers. I pestered my older brother to death and he would tolerate it for weeks or months before unleashing his fury on me to settle the score. In the same way, the Gilbert brothers fought on a regular basis, as did the Knight brothers. The one thing I remember about my brother was our parents leaving us home alone and the two of us getting into a fight, with me doing the ole hit and run technique: I would get a hit in and run for dear life. Hunter was much larger and stronger, but fortunately I was faster. If I could beat him to one of our exterior doors, I could make it into the yard and behind a car before getting caught. Then I could run circles around the car so he couldn't catch me. He would be livid and try for a while before getting frustrated, at which point he would just go back into the house and lock all the doors, leaving me outside to fend for myself until one of our parents came home. When they arrived, I would walk in with them as though nothing had happened and we would soon forget about it and move on, as brothers should. To this day, I can still remember how it felt to have my heart beating out of my throat as I ran from him, knowing that if I were ever caught I was going to take a beating, a well-deserved one at that.

In addition to neighborhood fun, there were hunting, fishing, and golfing outings with Daddy. We did these activities a dozen times or so until I was about ten years old. I believe I can remember every single instance. There was that time Daddy took all the neighborhood kids to a bream pond and we learned to hook crickets and worms to catch fish. Another time we went out on a boat with one of Daddy's friends, Jim Morton. It was freezing cold so everyone was miserable. I wanted to stay out so badly because I had never fished from a boat before, but misery won over and we went in early. Then there was the hunting. Daddy was an avid quail hunter, and I used to hunt alongside him and Papa Ed early in the morning throughout quail season, which had to have been in the winter because it was always freezing. They had many hunting dogs, English and Irish setters, pointers, and others. Daddy even had a hunting dog named Speck who was a legend because he had such a "soft mouth" he could retrieve a raw egg without breaking it. Daddy used to hustle people with this all the time by betting them that Speck could do this and then taking their money. Daddy would roll the egg out on the grass and Speck could get it in his mouth and bring it back without a crack.

I remember the first time I was allowed to shoot a shotgun, the first time I saw a bird dog on point, and the first time I got a real set of overalls. My overalls were some type of brown denim material, so Mama White took linoleum flooring and sewed it to the front portion of both legs so that the briars could not cut me up through the legs. When you could hunt for wild quail decades ago, you were forever walking through briars chest high on a little guy, so this overalls modification was great. After multiple years of going hunting without a gun because I was too small to shoot one, Daddy finally bought me a single shot, 20-gauge shotgun. I was so happy I didn't know what to do. It was like I had finally gotten my man card. Ironically and sadly, we went hunting only one time after I was given the gun and I never even got to shoot at a bird. Even so, hunting all morning with Daddy and Papa Ed and the dogs, then coming home to a massive breakfast made by Mama White was the best day a boy could experience. These were the absolute greatest of times for me because all my favorite people were there—Mother, Daddy, Papa Ed, and Mama White.

In addition to hunting and fishing, Daddy was an avid golfer and desperately wanted me and Hunter to play golf. He would try to help us in this any way that he could. One way he did this was to take us to a driving range. There wasn't one anywhere in the Gadsden area at that time, except maybe at the country club and we certainly couldn't go there. There was one, however, at the Lake Guntersville State Park public golf course, which was at least an hour away. Sometimes we would ride up there to hit balls and maybe play nine holes. There was a guy there named Bud who worked in the pro shop. As it turns out, Bud liked to drink a few Budweisers, and Guntersville County was a dry county at that time, meaning you couldn't buy or sell alcohol in the entire county. Every time we went, Daddy would get a half case of Budweiser and take it to Bud as he paid for the first bucket of balls. Then we could hit all the balls we wanted and even get in a few holes free of charge. Daddy always knew how to work a system.

ᥣ • ᥦ

These, and so many more were the really good memories from the days in our Alabama City neighborhood when I was very young. There were other memories, however, which are very painful. I know these kinds of memories are not unique to my childhood home, but at least in my neighborhood I think my house might have been the most severe. These are the memories of people you love hurting each other over and over again. The memories of hours upon hours of verbal fighting between my parents, memories of the police coming to our house to break up these fights because the neighbors had called them, memories of physical violence and unrelenting verbal abuse. I am over fifty years old as I write these words, and the images remain devastatingly clear in my mind.

These very frequent and frightening fights almost always started with Daddy coming home drunk. Not always, but usually. He was a bourbon man and would drink it straight out of the bottle with Coke as a chaser. As the night grew longer, he would want to go out to Fred and Jean's Lounge, or sometimes the Moose Lodge. These places were back-to-back on Wall Street, adjacent to the old cotton mill. With the Moose Lodge being a private club, it could remain open on Sundays, whereas Fred and Jean's had to close at two a.m. on Saturday night. For a decade or more, Daddy would want to go out to one of these hell holes, or was just getting back from one, and the fights would begin regarding who he was with all night and what he was doing. More often than not, he was with another lady and stayed out most of the night, if not all night, and everyone with eyes to see knew this to be the case. Spouses driven by love and wounded by insecurity, however, will always pretend to be blind, too frightened to honestly face reality. It is a terribly sad state of affairs when a violent manipulator is paired with an insecure spouse, as was the case in our house. It becomes a vicious cycle that no one seems capable of escaping, and the scenario happens all too often in our world.

The fights in our home would usually begin with some expletive-laced yelling. "You lazy mother fucker, you sit around here on your ass all day while I bust mine out there to provide this house and these cars," Daddy would yell.

"Well that doesn't give you the right to whore around all the damn time. You are a disgrace hanging out with all those whores at the Moose Lodge. Whores, tramps, and God knows what else. I wish you would just get your shit and get the hell out of here!"

"I ain't going a Goddamn place, this is my fucking house so if anybody leaves here it is going to be you, you lazy son of a bitch."

I know that shocks the eyes and the ears, but if anything, it is severely understated in its crass rudeness. And these were not five-, ten-minute fights! No, there would be yelling like this that went on for maybe thirty minutes to an hour or more, nonstop.

I remember lying in bed at night and kicking the wall hoping it would stop, totally unable to do anything other than lie there, cry, and listen. Tragically, there was generally only one way the fighting would come to an end—in violence. After enough insults had been hurled, Daddy would reach out and presumably grab Mother, usually by the hair, and threaten to really hit her. I didn't see this, mind you, as I was in my bed with the door tightly shut. But based on everything I would hear, I knew exactly what was happening.

When Daddy would grab her, Mother would yell out, "H.M., don't you hit me, H.M.! Stop, nooooo, please don't hurt me!"

"Then shut your fucking mouth and leave me alone!"

And in this way it would end, for that night anyway. It was tragic for everyone involved. For Mother, it was a never-ending cycle of manipulation and violence. She couldn't just let him sleep around and lay out all night without saying a word. When she laid into him, she was angry and hurled every insult she could think of at him. I often wondered why she never stopped engaging him in this way, but this was a boy she had known since sixth grade so she didn't really fear him until he got physical. For me and Hunter, it was a soul-wrenching experience to hear this battle between the two people we loved the most. Even for Daddy, it was him at his absolute worst because of the alcohol and anger, as he really did love us dearly and so lamented these violent years later in life. Without a doubt, it was simply tragic for everyone at 3704 Roselawn Drive.

❧ • ☙

When this type of conflict happens in front of you as a young boy, it does something to your soul that you only fully realize later in life. Men, by our very nature, are made to be protectors. We have an inherent code within our DNA that compels us to protect the weak. When the weak are injured or dominated by another in our presence and we either cannot or will not come to their aid, we feel a deep sense of guilt and shame. That is true when you are seven and it is true when you are seventy. When this type of thing is happening to you as a child and there isn't a single thing you can do about it because you are as scared of your father as anyone, it causes your soul to die a little. You learn to lie in bed and cry and curse your own father: "You sorry mother fucker, one day I am going to grow up and kick your ass for all of this!" Like father, like son. Other times you vacillate between praying to God and asking for Him to make this stop, or cursing at Him because He refuses to intervene. It is a vicious cycle that is impossible to appropriately process as a child.

What is even worse, with no one to confide in you begin to download really intense emotions and issues on similarly immature middle schoolers, your only other emotional outlet. I remember crying and telling a girl on whom I had a crush in sixth grade that I just wanted my dad "to run off with one of those whores and get out of here." Immediately after this, I could no longer stand to look at her or talk with her because of the shame I felt in admitting to weakness by crying while telling her. Even worse, she now knew the "family secret," so every time I saw her I felt intense shame, not because of anything I had done, but because she *knew*. This secret, among others, was one that we were never explicitly told to hide, but nevertheless knew we had to hide at all costs. The fear of this girl exposing us and telling others our secrets was crippling; fortunately she never did tell.

This type of secret family abuse is a lot more common than most want to believe. As a pastor of more than twenty years, I have seen and heard it too many times. As an adult who survived it for most of my childhood, I have only recently developed the wisdom, experience, and vocabulary to articulate exactly what happened and how it impacts the soul of a child. One thing it does is skew your sense of shame. As an adult, I have an incredibly high shame meter, not only for what I do, but for what everyone else does. If another person, even a stranger, is doing something shameful, I feel their shame for them. Not only that, but I often don't respond with compassion to these feelings of shame, but rather with anger. My anger, which was bottled up all those years while lying on my bed and begging Daddy to stop, comes flying out. I hate the feeling of shame so much I try to destroy it instantaneously everywhere it exists. That is why I am such a perfectionist and can never just look at myself in the mirror and say, "You missed that one Todd, don't worry about it and get the next one." I can tell others that all day long with conviction, but I can never say it to myself and believe it because it feels shameful to be wrong, make a mistake, or let someone down.

I only began to understand this concept when I was in my late twenties in seminary. I had a counseling professor who took an interest in me and began to help me unpack some of my emotional baggage. Once he sat me down in front of a blank piece of paper and said, "Write down for me every emotion that you have experienced." I wrote down happy, mad, angry. That was it, that was my full emotional vocabulary at about twenty-seven years of age. I was shocked when he said there are at least forty words I should be able to put on that paper. I thought he was kidding until he started naming them—fear, guilt, shame, helplessness, sadness, pride, determination, joy, contentment. Even now, I have to look those emotions up on Google to remind me of what they are, as I can't remember them and don't readily feel things other than happy, mad, angry, or sad. These things are set early in childhood and they can be retarded in their growth by trauma such as I experienced, or they can be accentuated in their growth by appropriate nurture. If you were nurtured well and feel a broad range of emotions deeply, go and praise your parents and bless them, as that is a great gift. On the other hand, if your emotional avenues were stunted by trauma and shame, get yourself in the company of folks that are emotionally and spiritually healthier than you so that you can grow in these areas rather than staying in the dysfunctional place where you were left as a child.

Besides these "normal" fights that seemed to happen all the time, there were others that were exceptional and especially frightening. Once, my parents were fighting and Mother took me and Hunter out of our beds while telling us we were leaving and going to her parents' house in Hollypond, about an hour away. It was late, maybe midnight, and we had already been in bed for a while. Daddy was really drunk and sitting on the couch, which he almost never did. He had a recliner and that was his seat, the Chief's throne, but tonight he was on the couch and we were in the hallway, twenty feet away, about to rush out the front door. Mother was yelling something at him when he smirked, reached into his jacket, pulled out a pistol, and pointed it at us. I can still see his face with that drunken smirk. There we were, crammed in a four-foot-wide hallway only ten feet from the front door. Mother yelled bloody murder and we all ran for the door. Somehow, we didn't even wind up going to her parents that night and soon went back inside the house, though I don't remember anything beyond us rushing out of the house. When I wrote this story down for this book, I actually called Hunter and asked him, "I am pretty sure this happened, but I need you to confirm that because I have never spoken about this to anyone and I want to make sure it really happened." He confirmed that it happened. It was the first time in forty years either of us had ever mentioned it. I don't believe for one minute that Daddy would have hurt us intentionally, but he was drunk out of his mind and in that state he was a master intimidator. He was clearly saying to Mother, "Leave me the hell alone!" It certainly could have been tragic, but fortunately the gun didn't go off.

Another evening Hunter and I were outside playing in the yard. I was probably about seven or eight years old. All of a sudden, Chief came out onto the porch and yelled to us to come inside. Hunter must have run as he was the first one in. Before I could reach the door, Mother came busting out of the front door and grabbed me, yelling, "Don't you go in there, your Daddy is crazy!" She picked me up in her arms and started hysterically yelling at Daddy, saying, "You send Hunter out here right now H.M. Don't you keep him in there, you let me have him."

Of course, Daddy would not comply and probably flipped her off, as he was prone to do. I have no idea what they were fighting about, but it must have been about custody of us in some form. Mother wound up with me in her arms while Chief had Hunter inside. Mother was probably 120 pounds soaking wet, but when it came to her kids she was a mama grizzly bear that would fight you. After yelling and crying and getting hysterical in the front yard, Mama Zana's big Buick pulled up and into the single-car garage, which we never used for parking. Somehow Mother knew what was happening and she took a bucket and put a brick or rock in it and swung it around like discus, letting it go so that it crashed right through our living room bay window, yelling for Hunter the entire time. Just then Mama Zana's car pulled away with Hunter in it and I remember thinking we might be separated forever. I felt sorry for Hunter being with Mama Zana instead of being with Mother, as we weren't really close to Mama Zana and didn't really enjoy being at her house, and now I was afraid he might have to live there. Mother and I wound up at the Knights' house, one of our neighbors, and the police came out to straighten everything up as usual. I think we might have slept at the Knights' that night, but we were all back home the next day living as though nothing happened, with the only evidence being a piece of cardboard in our bay window.

The final incident that stays with me to this day was the time that I actually tried to stand up for Mother. I was probably somewhere between ten and twelve years old. Daddy had been on a long drinking binge, staying out all night for multiple nights. For some reason, I was home alone with Daddy while Mother and Hunter were out somewhere. By this age, I was well aware of Daddy's multiple affairs with other ladies and it was offensive to me. I loved Mother, and to see her hurt in these ways was maddening. I don't remember exactly how, but I knew Daddy was calling one of his girlfriends on his business line in the den. He had told me to go to the back of the house so he could make a call. As he dialed, I walked right back into the living room, only about fifteen feet from where he was on the phone. He told me to leave again and I shook my head no. It was a crazy courageous act for a boy, but I wanted to stop him from calling one of these ladies from the lounge. When I shook my head no, you would think he would have put the phone down, whipped my behind, and put me in my room. That is what I expected, but he did something totally different, something totally unexpected. He just looked at me and said, "Fine, but if you tell your Mother I will kick your ass!" Then he proceeded to dial the number and the lady answered on the other end. He immediately asked her, "Where the hell were you last night, I was there waiting for you?" She replied something and then he said something along the lines of, "Don't you ever pull that shit again, you hear me?" The conversation went on for a little while, but all I remember was standing there trying to defend my mother's honor. I didn't stop the call from happening, but I was a silent witness in opposition to it. It was probably the only time I ever resisted Chief as a young boy during these dark days.

૭ૐ • ૐ૭

Tragically, there were other similar events that frightened me, but they caused much more pain and hysteria in my mother's life since she always got the brunt of his anger. Reflecting back on that time now, I can't fully explain it. Daddy was not an evil man and I know he loved us, but he was sick. He was emotionally lost, painfully addicted, and prone to extreme mood swings. In this state, when the whiskey came in and removed the filter from his broken and angry soul, there was hell to pay, and Mother was the one there to pay it. Oh, how I wish she would have left him early in their marriage, for his sake as well as hers. Yet she was fragile and insecure, with very deep emotional scars that kept her from believing she could make it without him, so she stayed no matter the cost.

For his part, he manipulated her continually by telling her that she could never make it financially without him and that if she ever left him and took us boys, he would never help her and she would wind up "living in those goddam projects," the government housing complex which was exclusively African American at the time and in segregated Gadsden that was an incredibly frightening thought for a white mother of two boys. I heard that refrain a dozen times and Mother heard it even more. Much later in life, when I was in my last few years of high school or early college, I remember begging Mother to "take all Daddy's shit and put it out in the front yard and be done with him and I will take care of you." At this time, he was having a well-publicized and long-standing affair with another lady in our town and it was an embarrassment to all of us. Mother, however, was so broken-down emotionally that she could agree with me in principle, but didn't have the emotional energy to even contemplate such a move. When a woman is in this type of abusive relationship, she generally has to get out early. The longer she stays, the more her self-esteem and confidence are broken and the less likely she is to ever have enough emotional energy to start over alone. It is so tragic.

While studying for my Masters degree, I relayed just a small amount of this to my psychology professor and asked him, "What in the world causes a man to physically and verbally abuse a lady like this, one he obviously doesn't want to leave or he would have already left!" I couldn't understand it. Daddy loved me and Hunter, and he loved Mother in some ways, he was just an emotional and spiritual mess that abused her horrifically.

My psychology professor replied, "To be honest, we really don't know, but when we get as close as we can to the truth in these scenarios, it is generally a very perverted way of saying, 'Don't leave me!'" He went on to explain that emotionally damaged men can get really insecure themselves so they actually abuse their wives out of fear their wives will leave them, believing that they can break them down to the point to where they can't leave. This is exactly what happened in our house. Then he said the words that were so sad to me. "If only these men would embrace the fact that they don't have to keep their wives from leaving via abuse and fear, love and companionship would certainly make their wives desire to be loyal."

"Beat her down or she will leave you," says the Devil. "Love her and honor her and she will love and honor you," says the Lord. The Devil always motivates out of fear and pushes an agenda of selfish abuse, while the Lord always has an agenda of love and motivates us to serve others freely, not trap them. True love is never motivated by fear, it is motivated by gratitude. I don't know that my mother ever really experienced that type of love and that tragedy breaks my heart.

Episodes such as these in the lives of children become hidden and destructive family secrets. Since no one knows quite what to say about them, nobody ever says anything. Therefore, it gets emotionally buried and often never mentioned, or only mentioned some forty years later as in my case. This type of scenario is all too common in our world today and it is why this book and many others like it need to be written. Those of us who have experienced these things and worked through them over decades need to share our journeys with others so that they can in turn speak about their own trauma with those closest to them and begin the healing process.

Carnes family (circa 1977)

Me and my brother, Hunter

CHAPTER 5

MILL VILLAGE CHARACTERS

O ne of the most interesting things looking back at my mill village roots are the unique characters I grew up around. In a small mill village area like Alabama City, there was a never-ending litany of interesting folks who were a big part of my early life.

First of all, there was Wendell. He was a carpenter who worked for my dad all through my childhood. Looking back, Wendell was a really sick man who was a dire alcoholic, though that term was never used. People just called them *drunks* back then and joked about it. Wendell was married to Beatrice, a very large and intimidating lady who drove a school bus in the neighboring city of Attalla. I don't know that Wendell ever had a driver's license, or perhaps he lost it due to DUIs, so it was always my job to go and get him and take him home. Daddy always said that Wendell was one of the best carpenters he knew and that he could have been great if he hadn't stayed drunk all the time. That was a recurring theme in my world, folks that had the potential to be great at something but the "whiskey got 'em."

I remember even as a sixteen-year-old kid, I used to feel sorry for Wendell. He was a hard worker and always very kind to me and to most everyone. He had a really rough life, living in a small shack on the side of a hill that he had probably built himself. He was missing most of his teeth, was never shaved, and was very short in stature. I still remember the manners he would use with the home-owners when he would humbly ask for a glass of water while we worked all day in the hot Alabama summers. I always felt sorry for him because of the way most folks constantly made fun of him for his drunkenness and gossiped that his wife would whip him when he came home too drunk, and there were often marks to prove it. A construction site in the mill village is a ruthless and unforgiving place, where the strong prey on the weak, and Wendell got more than his fair share of abuse. I, however, always liked and appreciated him because he would try and teach me things on the job and I never saw him abuse another. Even a child recognizes good and evil.

Next in line was George, a really nice guy who let me do a lot of things on the job others wouldn't allow, like running a table saw or a skill saw on a ladder. He would also lay out walls and let me swing that sixteen-ounce framing hammer for hours driving those sixteen-penny nails, as this was long before there were nail guns. At this time, you had races to see how many licks it would take you to drive a sixteen-penny nail. Once you got really good, you could set it with one lick and drive it with two more. Some folks could even set it with one lick and drive it with the second, but to do that you had to really set it hard with that first lick while holding it with your left hand. If you missed, you would hit your thumb so hard that it would hurt for days and then you would lose your thumbnail. I was always content to drive them with three licks and save my thumb after having destroyed it a few times.

George will be remembered for multiple things, but primarily as the guy who could cuss in more decorative ways than anyone Hunter and I had ever known, Chief included. He could put together a string of cuss words a mile long and reveled in doing so. He also had his own lectionary of phrases that he taught me related to carpentry work. There were things like, "That'll be fine once we get some of that one-inch caulk out here" when I would cut wrong and leave a big gap. There was another one he would use when something was not great, but good enough: "That'll look fine by the time we get to Fred and Jean's Lounge this afternoon." When he was ready for you to drive something he was holding for you, he would always say, "Don't just stand there, hit that son of a bitch." Yep, George had a mouth on him, but he was as gentle as they come and a really good carpenter. Daddy liked him and entrusted him with the difficult jobs. George lived with a lady in town, whom Daddy affectionately labeled Sweet Thang. George would generally work for a year or so and then totally disappear for a few months. Daddy always thought he was driving a semi-truck during these breaks, maybe because he broke up with Sweet Thang. He did this for years and it was just kind of a running joke among us until one day we opened the paper to see George on the front page, but they weren't calling him George. They called him Scott and he was in handcuffs as a fugitive from justice who had been on the run for more than a decade!

It turned out George had been tried and convicted of murder many years ago and had somehow escaped from the Alabama penitentiary. He had been on the run using an alias and moving around just enough to avoid capture. Strangely enough, he remained in the same state where he committed the murder.

Earlier in his life, George had been married to a lady and he was a long-haul trucker. He had suspicions his wife was cheating on him, so he left one day for a supposed week-long trip, drove about a mile away, and stopped. He parked his truck and walked back to his house to see if his suspicions were correct. Unfortunately, they were. He walked right in on his wife in the bed with a deputy sheriff. I don't know where the deputy's gun was, but he was now caught naked in the bed with George's wife in George's own home. There is no greater disrespect than that. George had a claw hammer in his hand and he beat the poor man to death with it right there in his own bedroom. It had to be gruesome and none of us could imagine George doing anything like that, but that level of disrespect in a blue-collar mill town can be a death sentence since a man's pride is often all he owns and he will certainly fight for it. George was convicted of second-degree murder and given a life sentence, but somehow escaped prison. He was then able to live on the run for more than a decade, but now he was sent back to the penitentiary and never got out as far as I know. Daddy went down to his parole hearings faithfully for many years, always to no avail.

There was Glen "Eyeball Drywall," the sheetrock man. He used me as labor when he was hanging ceilings, as that is a two-person job. Once, we were sent out to repair a ceiling that was water damaged and literally bowl shaped due to the water that had been above it. As we got on either edge to start to take it apart, Glen took a great swing on his side and dropped an entire ceiling on my head. Fortunately, it was brittle and busted up upon impact, but I probably breathed in several pounds of insulation trying to escape the room.

Larry was another, a 1950s-throwback guy who always had slicked-back hair, long in the back with Elvis Presley "pork chop"–style sideburns. He always drove a 1950s hotrod car and not an old pickup truck like everyone else, which I thought was really cool.

Datsun was the carpet layer. He was a short man but had the biggest arms I have ever seen, and according to Daddy, he would hurt you. I still remember Daddy telling me about Datsun getting into a fight at Fred and Jean's and taking a pool ball and cramming it into the mouth of another guy with a solid jab, knocking out his front teeth. He certainly looked the part and now that I think about it, he looked and talked just like Ed Orgeron, the famous football coach at LSU.

Apart from the guys on the jobsite, there was Johnny, a young man with special needs who lived near Mama Zana in the mill village proper. Johnny had a sister named Trudy, also with special needs. I was always told that they were both born with physical and mental disabilities because their parents were close kin, cousins or half siblings, though it was never fully explained to me nor did I ever see their parents. Johnny would faithfully come over to my grandmother's house many evenings unannounced to sit and talk to her and my Aunt Juanita. He would tell them about his "girlfriends" and his plans in life and they would treat him with kindness. Knowing that area of town, I would bet that this was some of the rare kindness he received in life. Trudy would come as well and I vaguely remember her getting pregnant and coming over with her baby at some point. We all were anxious when Trudy made the announcement; we didn't know how or if she could care for a child.

The final person I have to mention would be Geraldine. She was an African American woman who would come to clean our house from time to time as Mother's health deteriorated. Geraldine couldn't drive either so that meant we would always go to pick her up and bring her to clean the house. In Gadsden at this time, there were areas of town where white people lived and areas where Black people lived. During the day, whites would go to the Black section of town for business and vice versa, but by nightfall everyone generally kept to their own side of town. This was somewhat of an unwritten rule. Since Daddy did most of his work in the Black section of town, he never went on appointments or to jobs past dark. And I don't ever remember any Black person being in our white neighborhood other than Geraldine.

Geraldine was always very anxious and nervous and jumpy. In fact, she would scare so easily that you had to be careful not to walk up on her without announcing yourself from a distance or she would yell and jump in fear. Daddy knew this and often tortured her by sneaking up on her and yelling "Boo!" She would jump out of her skin. It used to always bother Daddy that Geraldine would not ride in a car alone with him, as she would not get into a car with any man. I don't know if this was just a rule she had for white men or for men in general. So whenever he went to pick her up or take her home, he had to take one of us along. It was demeaning to him that she would take this stance, this woman he was hiring and paying who wouldn't ride the fifteen minutes with him to get to his home. I am sure it felt like she was accusing him of being a rapist and he resented it deeply, and I think that is why he caused her so much grief.

I fully understand this scenario because I had the same thing happen to me when I lived in Cyprus, and Kerri, my wife, was in the hospital for two months. I was raising our eighteen-month-old daughter alone at our temporary home and we hired a local housekeeper to help me out. She was Moldovan and also would not come to our home and work if I was there alone. My first reaction to this was just like Daddy's—I was appalled this woman was accusing me of hiring her as some type of ruse in order to rape her. I was a Christian missionary, after all! After cooling down and actually thinking it through, what I understood even at that young age was that she was not accusing me. Rather, I was guilty by association as part of the patriarchy of men that has a horrid reputation when it comes to manipulating and assaulting women they employee. By taking this stance, she was simply responding to her previous life experience, which had taught her that men in general are not safe and should not be trusted.

I hate to say it, but my life experience confirms her assessment of men in general. This will certainly offend the majority of men who are neither sexually nor physically dangerous to women, but if being offended is all that happens to them they need to step up and defend the women around them rather than giving tacit approval to "the way things are."

Dwight Manufacturing Cotton Mill

Dwight Manufacturing mill village homes

CHAPTER 6

DEATH'S UNINVITED ENTRANCE

I once read that whenever we are faced with death, our minds immediately want to drift back to our childhood to gain strength. This natural pull is why we get so much emotional support from our childhood friends and close relatives during times of crisis. My theory on why our mind wants to go back to childhood is that the mind is trying to escape the painful reality of death by returning to that time when we were conscious and enjoying life but had not yet experienced death; when the harsh reality of death had not yet entered our conscience reality and life was so much lighter. Once you experience that first death in life, you have now crossed a line in the sand that changes everything. It is your first existential lesson in your own mortality and the finality of death.

For some, this happens very early, and for others they make it well into their twenties or further before they are introduced to death's sting. Regardless, the deaths we experience as children powerfully shape our lives.

The first death I remember is the death of Chief's stepdad, Roy Smith. I knew Roy as a child, but we were never close. When he died, my dad called me while I was out with friends to let me know and I didn't even come home. Despite our close proximity to each other, his passing was not one that I felt deeply. The first death that really impacted me was the death of my best friend on September 10, 1987. His name was Jason Brown, but we just called him JC Cool. He was athletic, confident, popular, charismatic, and always had a knack for being at the right place at the right time. I don't think there was a single soul in our town that didn't like him. We had become really good friends during my junior year, which was great for me because it elevated my social status by three to four levels at least. We played basketball together, went drag racing in his three-speed Camaro, got Brian Bosworth mullet haircuts, and on and on. My nickname was Hot Dog, and my friends were Bullet, Dork, Chub, Boss, Hook, Hawk, Goose, Dope Smoker, Duck, and others, as a nickname was an absolute necessity in Gadsden. My nickname had its roots in the fact that some people mistakenly thought I might have taken a few too many shots on the basketball court, so I was given this nickname by David Mabrey, aka Duck.

Jason and I had become good friends and our girlfriends had become friends as well, so we spent even more time together. One night when I was seventeen, Jason called me at my girlfriend's house and asked if I could come pick him up from his girlfriend's house and take him home. He had lost his license a while back via a DUI and was without a vehicle. As I often did, I went and picked him up and we went back to his house and had a few beers. It was about one a.m. when we finished. I went home, as I knew Chief was going to wake me up at six-thirty a.m. to work for George or Wendell or Eyeball Drywall. After leaving that night, I never saw him again. As I remember, I went back over to his house at about four p.m. the following day after work and rode by a house with an ambulance in the street very near his house. That was when someone told me Jason had been electrocuted and they were working to try and revive him in the yard. They wouldn't let me get near the scene, but eventually they put him in an ambulance and rushed off to the hospital. I followed behind the ambulance. I was so shaken, I took a wrong turn and lost the ambulance, but arrived soon after the others. As I entered into the hospital, his mom or dad, I don't remember which, simply said, "Hot Dog (my nickname), he is gone." They asked if I wanted to go back and see him, which I did. I couldn't believe he was gone. Fourteen hours previously we were on his porch drinking beer and talking, as we did most nights after leaving our girlfriends' houses. His mom and dad asked if I would go pick up his little brother, Justin, from football practice, and tell him the tragic news while bringing him to the hospital.

I took off in my 1985 Monte Carlo for our high school, Emma Sansom, and went straight to the field house. I was crying and a mess when I burst in to get Justin. I don't remember how I phrased it, but I brought him to the car and told him Jason was gone. I remember being in such a state of shock and denial that even after I told Justin his brother was dead, I began to doubt myself. I began to think, "Maybe he is not dead? Maybe I am mistaken and I just thought he was dead and misunderstood." I was having these thoughts all the way back to the hospital, where the harsh reality was reaffirmed. JC Cool was dead at the age of eighteen and the sting of death entered my life unannounced and unwanted. Jason's death shocked our entire community, as he was honestly the most likable kid ever. More importantly for me and others, his death took us from immortal eighteen-year-olds to mortal eighteen-year-olds.

I remember so many things about that time, as your mind is in so much pain the memories get burned into it. The morning after his death I woke up and for a couple seconds it was like he was alive and I felt normal and happy. Then reality came crushing in and I felt the full force of the pain anew, just as if he died all over again. This early morning torture happened every day for several weeks. On the very first day after his death Daddy came into my room and hugged me. That was something he very rarely did, but he hugged me tight and told me that today was going to be horrible, but tomorrow would be a little better and then the next day would be a little better, and over the course of weeks and months I would make it through this tragedy. It was great advice. Daddy also lost a close friend at about the same age. He said they were out drinking one night and he went home early while his friend went back out for a little more fun. Later that night, his friend had a car wreck and died. He told me this story several times and he always said, "I never went home early, but this particular night I did and I have no idea why, but it saved my life."

Another occurrence that happened during this time is really unexplainable outside the realm of faith. Sometime during the week before Jason died he and I were sitting on five gallon buckets in one of the barns around his house, enjoying a dip of Copenhagen and talking about nothing. Then, out of the blue,

Jason said to me, "Hot Dog, we ought to go to church this Sunday."
"Church, why we goin' to church?" I replied. As an eighteen-year-old, I had been to a Sunday morning service no more than three or four times in my entire life, so that was not on my radar at all. Jason's family was a little more connected with a nearby church, but I don't know how often they attended. Feeling my hesitation, he replied, "Sure as hell won't hurt either one of us." I couldn't argue with that logic, so we agreed that we would go to church on Sunday. That was that and we moved on to other things, as talk about church wasn't anything we had ever discussed. Five days later, when he was no longer here to take me to that church service, these words became a source of both mystery and comfort and I will never forget them.

At Jason's funeral visitation, I distinctly remember Nardo bending over Jason's casket and kissing him on the forehead while crying violently. This stuck out to me because Nardo was black. We used to play basketball together and could be friendly on the basketball court, but only in that context. Off the court, black and white friendships were always fragile. Just a few months before Jason's death, Nardo's little brother stabbed one of our white friends at a gas station and punctured his lung. Who knows what the fight was about or how it got started, as it wasn't unusual to have a black versus white fight on a weekend. What was unusual was while they were carrying our friend off in the ambulance, Nardo and Jason almost came to blows in the rear of the service station while the police were still on the scene!

Incidents such as these just accentuate the weird cultural irony that all of us had to live through during this time. Integration was the law, but segregation was the reality in every sphere other than schools as we sorted through this time of transition. This meant we would have Black friends from school, primarily through athletic teams, and these friendships were real. However, we all also knew these friendships were only viable while there was peace between "our people and their people." This meant people like Nardo and Jason genuinely liked each other and were friends, as evidenced by Nardo's strong and painful reaction to Jason's death. Yet they also divided up very easily when it came to racial violence of any kind. Society was not ready for full integration, so we all lived with the knowledge that these friendships had to remain an inch deep so they could be easily broken if and when the fights started.

The feeling of sheer agony I felt walking away from the cemetery after Jason's burial will never be far from my mind. The finality of death had changed everything for me and many others. For months afterward, my life spiraled. I was drinking more and more, I was aimless and very depressed. More nights than I can count, I would go out drinking and partying and on the way home I would wind up at the graveyard by myself at two or three a.m., sitting on the grass at Jason's grave crying and talking to him. Most of my free time I spent at his house with his mom and brother and sister. They were obviously grieving so I felt at home in their house, as mine was filled with anger and depression. One night, several days after Jason was buried, an evangelist came to town and many of my friends went to hear him. I have no idea who dragged them there, as that was not the norm for anyone I knew. I didn't go. I had never really been in church and was uncomfortable when I had to be there for something. That night many of my friends had a real "come to Jesus" party, with several of them making spiritual decisions that would guide them the rest of their lives. Others made decisions that night that didn't really bring about change at that time, but was probably at least a small step in the right direction. Death had brought a sobering effect to all of our lives.

During this chaos, I often contemplated the ultimate issue of where I was going when it was all over for me. I believed in heaven and hell and knew I was hell-bound, so I honestly contemplated what it would mean to walk away from the crazy lifestyle of immorality, alcohol, and drugs, to give my life over to the Jesus I had read about as a young child. I counted the cost and almost made a decision to clean up and follow Jesus, but in the end the price was simply too high. I was a nobody when I was started middle school, but through my partying and "big personality," I had ascended to the upper echelons of the social pecking order and there was no way I could let that go, which I knew was required in order to follow Jesus. In other words, I loved the things of the world so much there was no way I could leave all of that and love the pure and holy things of God. I looked intently at the straight-and-narrow path that leads to life, then turned away and went back to wallow in the mud and mire of the wide path that leads to destruction, with my buddies.

There was another death soon after Jason's. It was the death of Chris Baswell. He was a year older than me and I knew him, but we weren't really close. He was out one night with a Camaro full of people. His Camaro was souped-up and he was known to drive hard and fast without fear. I remember being in his back seat one night and he was driving so fast that even though I was drunk, I was praying to myself, "God, if I die please don't send me to hell, please save me, please get me out of this." I made all kinds of promises to God in that car that night, all of which were soon forgotten once I got my feet back on solid ground. On another night, however, Chris was out driving and his car got away from him, and he, along with several others, were killed. There was only one survivor. Another death, another funeral, another moment that was screaming to me and many others that we are mere mortals who should make peace with God. Our ears, however, were so full of "party wax" that we refused to hear.

As if that weren't enough, just months later I was driving and was involved in an automobile accident that took the life of another man. It was a tragedy and one of the most frightening events of my life. Because of the fatality, it was thoroughly investigated and there was real talk of charges being brought against me. I'll never forget spending most of the night at the police station during the investigation with only Chief there with me. At the time, I was 6'1" and 165 pounds soaking wet, so adult prison in Alabama would not have been a kind place for me, as it was pure survival of the fittest at that time.

I have no idea of the truth about these things, but I had grown up with the stories of one of Chief's friends who went to the state penitentiary. Daddy always said that his friend told him how "he became the homosexual partner of the biggest, baddest dude in the place so that he would only be raped by one man. Otherwise he would be raped by a bunch of guys." These were just matter-of-fact statements passed on to me when I was in middle school about the realties of prison at that time, and I don't have any reason to doubt them.

So this is where I found myself at eighteen years of age. I had buried my best friend because of a freak electrical accident, buried a second friend as a result of a car accident, and now I was involved in an accident that took the life of yet another man. To say these days were dark is the ultimate understatement.

During this painful and tragic season, Chief stepped up for me in ways I will never forget. I desperately needed a coach who could help me navigate all of this death and destruction that had so violently entered my life over the last few months, as I was totally unprepared to handle it myself as an eighteen-year-old. As a father should, Chief stepped in and literally carried me through this dark valley. Around twenty-five years later, I found myself sitting with Chief in his house, just the two of us. We were talking and I told him that I would never forget his kindness and mercy during this very dark season of my life and that it was forever etched in my memory how he carried me during these days. He broke down crying and said, "Thank you, son." He then got up to give me a hug in tears. I remember I felt so proud to honor him in this moment and to remind him of some of the great things he did as a father during my darkest night, as it is all too easy to only remember our loved ones' mistakes and not their victories. I am so glad I had this moment with Chief, it was my way of beginning to give him my blessing. Thankfully, this incident was the final event of this "death defining" season of life, a season that fully introduced me to my own mortality and the concept of eternity.

Looking back, it is easy to see that any sane man would have run to the church and begged for mercy after all of these events. Obviously, I was not sane and I had no connection to any church other than the one where I sometimes played basketball. I was still that young boy who had lost so much of my manhood before I even reached puberty by witnessing the abuse in my house. I was mellow on the outside, yet bitterly angry on the inside. Just like Chief, this anger came out when I drank to excess, allowing my true feelings and emotions to escape. I was broken, alone, angry, directionless. I went to class at Gadsden State sometimes, I eked out decent grades and drank all of my cares and feelings away from Thursday afternoon through Sunday morning. It was a vicious cycle that was only going to end in one of three ways: jail, the grave, or a radical change. A seed of righteousness had definitely been planted in my soul when Jason died, but it had not yet been watered sufficiently to germinate and grow.

Jason Brown, Trey Taylor and me at high school graduation, three months before Jason's death

Jason's Obituary

CHAPTER 7

ADDICTION OF THE FATHER

" Son, I ain't ever known a Carnes that wasn't a drunk, so you are crazy as hell for getting out here and starting that drinking shit with these boys. We ain't like other people, Son, we get started and we can't stop! And you wanna know what the worst thing is about getting drunk? You always cuss the people you love the most."

Daddy didn't just tell this to me once in my life, he told it to me multiple times as I came home somewhere between buzzed and sloppy drunk. Sometimes he would poke his finger in my chest and threaten me with a grown-man ass whoopin' in the backyard, other times he would sit calmly at the kitchen table and plead with me, "Son, I am not saying I am smarter than you are, I've just been down this road already." At the time, neither approach worked because I was young, arrogant, and determined to go down the well-worn path of addiction just like all the other

Carnes, and there would be hell to pay.

I don't know all of the scientific data related to addiction, but research from the National Institutes of Health (NIH) has proven some genetic predisposition that makes some more vulnerable than others.[2] I don't, however, believe that is the source of it all. I think environment, relationships and trauma come into play as well. In 2015, Dr. Marco Venniro of the National Institute on Drug Abuse looked at the roots of addiction in relation to social acceptability and interaction.[3] His study required rats to choose between social interaction with another rat or access to a drug (heroin or meth-amphetamine). The animals consistently chose social interaction when given the choice. This was the case when they were first given access to one of the drugs and when they were experienced drug users. The conclusion is obvious. Addiction is a function of relational disconnectedness. If life is painful and lonely, substance abuse is a ready-made escape. On the other hand, even when life is painful and stressful, this pain and stress can be "medicated" with friends and community support as easily as it can be medicated with mind-numbing substances. Of course the issue is multifaceted, but I can easily see how this is a significant part of the equation that leads to addiction. Unfortunately, this disastrous cycle played itself out in my family generation over generation.

In my father's case, he had a very tough "row to hoe," as we often say in the South. He grew up in the home of a single mother who cared for two children and two parents on one mill worker's wages, which made her poorer than poor. He was smart and athletic, but after his motorcycle accident and the ten months he spent

2   https://www.ncbi.nlm.nih.gov/pmc/articles/
PMC3506170/#::text=Twin%20studies%20have%20shown%20that,of%20
gene%20%C3%97%20environment%20interaction.
3   https://www.drugabuse.gov/about-nida/noras-blog/2018/
10/new-nida-research-reveals-power-social-reinforcers

at the children's hospital in Birmingham as a fifteen-year-old boy, he was changed. He was in a full body cast (from his chest to his feet) for multiple months and lost all of his lower body strength. Perhaps the worst part of it all—he was there alone. His mom and stepfather had to work to keep food on the table even with their son in the hospital for months on end.

I can't imagine the loneliness Daddy experienced during these days. He missed the entire year of school so he fell back a grade, but more tragically he lost his ability to play high school sports. Daddy watched other kids come and go from Children's Hospital for almost a year. He used to tell me stories about how the burn victims would come in and they would have to be "picked" as part of their healing process. As I understand it, a "picking" was a process whereby kids were put in a tub of sorts and scabs were picked off of their healing bodies. He said their cries and yells were horrific and haunted him. He talked about other kids who were brought there with polio who were placed in iron lungs, destined to lie on their backs and look up at a mirror to see anything happening around them for the rest of their lives because the disease had paralyzed their lungs. It was a place full of tragedy, and he was there alone at the age of fifteen to process these things in addition to his own life-altering disability and deformities.

Eventually, he began to realize that he was much better off than so many others who were there and this began to restore some of his optimism. When he returned home, he remained homebound for several months. The multiple operations on his left foot actually succeeded in providing him with a foot that worked, though his ankle joint was locked in place, never to move again. All things considered, this would have been a decent solution had he not been still growing. His healthy leg continued to grow while his newly rebuilt leg stopped. This left him with one leg about three inches shorter than the other, so he wore a built-up shoe the rest of his life with a brace around the calf. I can only imagine the pain and embarrassment this caused him as a teenager, but he managed to muscle through it and do whatever he wanted. I remember when I was a boy I saw a set of wooden skis in our garage where the shoe on the left ski was built up three inches higher than the other. Chief could not only water ski, but he could ski jump! Rumor has it he was also a good dancer, and he obviously had enough balance to be a decent street fighter as he had more than a few of those.

This was Chief's childhood tragedy, along with his father's complete abandonment of the family. So here you have a young man who was deprived of his father, who then made some real progress in life only to see it all taken away with a horrific accident that would leave him literally limping the rest of his life. Even more, he spent ten months alone in a hospital bed seventy miles from home. That is a tough start to life. Now that I am older, I can easily appreciate the damage this type of childhood would have on a young man. It would bring about insecurity regarding your place and acceptance in the world of the 1950s. (He never used a handicap sticker in his life nor did he ever use the term.) Anger about the injustices of life, how the driver of the car might have been drunk and caused all this pain while seemingly never punished, were also his reality. Addiction became an easy lane in which to ride through it all, even though he knew the damage it had caused to his own family via his father. Unfortunately, as a way to cope and numb deep, real pain, addictions plagues families and people generation after generation.

I don't know when he started drinking, but definitely

sometime before college. I am sure, just like me, he found that he could "find another gear" socially when he was drinking, and that probably allowed him to cover up his insecurities and provide what we always called "liquid courage." Alcohol definitely delivers on that, but it does even more. It medicates the emotional pain while releasing the anger, and I am sure he had a lot of both. I know I did.

Addiction is also crafty in that it takes control very slowly. First, it is just a way to relax, lose some of your inhibitions, and have a good time. Then, for an addict, it becomes the *only* way you can have a good time. It becomes the actual substance of the good time. When you drink even more, it takes down the outer barrier you have built to restrain anger and cover shame and sadness. As the alcohol takes a larger and larger place in life, it pulls down the veil so that the raw emotion, usually anger, spills out like an erupting volcano, seemingly unprovoked. It has often been held in so long that as soon as the body is relaxed, the anger pours out. Unfortunately, as Daddy often said, it is most often visited upon those you love the most since they are the closest. Anger, though, is not the only emotion pent up in the soul of an addict. There is also sadness and shame, and they usually come out once the anger has dissipated. We called these "the sad drunks" back at home. The self-protective masks and coverings are laid bare and tears and apologies and deep regret finally come out, but are never taken seriously because everyone knows "he is just drunk." If you have experienced the angry, violent drunks, you have probably experienced the sad drunks that often follow, as they are often two sides of the same coin.

For Daddy, his emotions fell into a very predictable pattern during his decades of addiction. He would work himself silly for weeks on end, probably staying out late and sleeping little, but working every day. He was self-employed so he had some flexibility, but if he didn't work he didn't earn, so he had to get up and hustle. After multiple weeks, or maybe even a few months, the stress and the pressure would become too much and he would need to check out for a while. This is when he would run and hide in the bottle. He would start at one of the local lounges, staying there most of the night. He would then come home in the early morning and maybe sleep a few hours before rising the next morning to start drinking bourbon as hard as he could. During these first two days of drinking, he was angry as hell and mean as a snake. He would cuss those of us he loved, and bully us as well. He always had a recliner and about a day or two into his seven- to ten-day binge, he would make me come and sit on the arm of the recliner with him.

Always when he was drunk, and often when he was not, he would call me *asshole*. Not sometimes, always. I have no idea why. He didn't have that kind of name for my brother. I know this probably sounds weird, and looking back it is pretty demeaning, but it wasn't nearly as demeaning as it sounds now. As a child I was able to process that he was just drunk and drunks do stupid stuff, so I honestly didn't take offense, as *asshole* was one of the least offensive words thrown around inside the walls of 3704 Roselawn Drive. Furthermore, he loved me and I knew it, but he was definitely raw and crude when he was drinking.

What was dreadful, however, was hearing the words, "Come here, Asshole, and sit with yo' Daddy." I would dutifully go and sit on the arm of his recliner while he would talk and cuss and slur, saying all kinds of weird things that were demeaning to Mother, who was right there across from him on the couch. This only happened after the mean-as-hell first two days were past and he had transitioned to the sadness. If I resisted going to his chair to sit on the arm of it with him, the anger would flash and threats of real violence could come hurling out. The first few days of the sadness were tolerable, but by day five or six he hadn't bathed in a week and was just sitting there drinking and sleeping. By this time, he was rank and pitiful, even to an eight-year-old. He would repeat himself over and over, asking me obvious questions and forcing me to answer them again and again. Things like, "Here, grab this finger, Asshole. Do you think you are strong enough to break that finger? Answer me! You think you can break it? You better not." Then he would laugh eerily.

Other crazy things he'd say in this drunken haze were, "You know what your Daddy's gonna do tomorrow? I am going to get in that car and go to Pete's and get me a bottle of whiskey. You wanna go?" Pete was a bootlegger at the time and he was the place to get yourself a bottle of whiskey at night or on Sundays when the liquor store was closed. Pete was always open. He lived in this house that seemed haunted and you would go to the side door anytime, day or night, and knock. Eventually, a small outside light would come on and Pete would open the rickety screen door and stick out his head. I still remember his face. He had a head full of white hair and black, horn-rimmed glasses like they issue in the army. Once he made sure you were a friendly who actually had money and not the police, he would take your order. Then you made the exchange, cash for a brown-bagged pint of whiskey. Surely every officer in the county knew about this place, but in the mill village it wasn't worth the time or effort to keep hard working people from getting a bottle of whiskey when they wanted it. The officers might have used Pete as well on an occasional Sunday.

At some point in this predictable process, Mother would chime in with, "No, you are not going to get another pint of whiskey, you are going to sober up and go to work. We are tired of you sitting around here aggravating everybody."

"Ah, I'll do whatever the hell I want to do, woman, you shut your damn mouth. Tell her, Todd, tell her to shut up and let's go to Pete's." When he was saying crazy things like this, all I wanted to do was get up and go to my room. If you tried to leave before he was through with you, though, that is when you got the fury, as it was taken as a sign of disrespect.

During these times, I don't ever remember us going hungry or being without food, but I do remember worrying about it. Daddy would be drunk sometimes for several weeks and Mother would openly talk about us not having any money and her not knowing what to do about it. She would beg him to sober up and go to work, reminding him that we didn't have money. Some of his workers would also come to the house and talk about his current jobs not having materials on site; they would be wanting paychecks and we wouldn't have any money to pay them or buy materials. Sometimes one of them would take over and cover for Daddy for a few days, but oftentimes they were simply out of luck until he sobered up. Sobering up was a twenty-four to forty-eight-hour process after being drunk for a solid two weeks. He would sleep and throw up for a day or so trying to come back to life because everything was coming apart at the seams. When he did come back, he would hit the ground running to clean up all the mess that was out there with his subcontractors, material suppliers, and customers and somehow recover.

During these binges, Hunter and I would get our fair share of anger from Daddy, but the majority of his anger was pointed at

Mother. It was in the first few days of these binges that they would have those long cuss fights through the night. Multiple times I remember the police coming to break it up, but the majority of the time they just fought it out until the violence started, at which point Mother would start begging for him to "quit, don't you hit me H.M.!" It was pitiful to hear her beg and most of the time she only received a single slap or a hair pull or something to that effect, although she told me that Daddy once broke her nose and another time blacked her eyes. Following these episodes, it would calm down and we could finally go to sleep. Fortunately, this type of anger and abuse only lasted a few days before ushering in the sadness, which would last for the next week or two.

This is how the roots of addiction spread from my grandparents into my childhood home. These things are predictable from generation to generation even though every child who suffers under the violence and selfishness of an addicted parent surely makes promises that they will never do that to their children. I made those promises and I dare to guess that Chief did as well. As an eight-year-old boy trying to protect your mom and hating your dad's drunkenness, there is no possible way you can see yourself following in these footsteps and doing this to people you love. As a matter of fact, all you really want to do is grow up to be big enough to beat up your own father and make him stop.

Breaking free is not that simple. As children grows into their own teenage years, they have a decade of pent up anger, sadness, and shame. Most often they haven't had any way to process these things in a healthy manner and are generally in an environment where everybody drinks or smokes pot, etc. Thus, using an immature fifteen-year-old brain, you begin to self-medicate with alcohol and drugs, thinking it is just something for you to play with for this season of life and lay down later. You never dream that it could make you as mean or hostile as your father. Addiction, however, is incredibly deceptive. You always start off playing with your substance of choice and before you know it, the substance is playing with you. At fifteen you controlled it, at eighteen it controls you. Now you are caught in the cycle of drunkenness, foolish behavior, and bad outcomes, which leads to intense shame. This shame then has to be medicated with drunkenness and the cycle continues in a horrific downward spiral. In my case, as in others', I honestly couldn't believe I had very subtly become just like my father, doing the very types of things I absolutely despised as a child.

This was impressed upon me in a way I would like to forget, but never will. One night when I was in the deep throes of addiction, I was at home and a guy called and said he was coming over to fight me, a dispute over a girl, of course. I began to put on my shoes to get outside and take on this fight in my front yard when the young lady in question, who was at my house at the time, told my mother what was about to happen. When Mother heard this, she started yelling hysterically. Unfortunately for the other guy, Daddy was right at the door and went barreling out ahead of me. The guy pulled up and opened his door just as I stepped outside. Before I could get off the porch, Daddy had grabbed him by the shirt as he exited his car and then threatened to knock his teeth out. I came right behind, but by the time I got there the guy was in his car and getting the heck out of dodge. I decided all of this was the young lady's fault, so I poured out all of my pent-up anger upon her in our front yard. I was both frustrated and ashamed that Daddy caught the guy before I got there, preventing me from proving my toughness to Chief. My anger exploded with curses and all kinds of insults. I have never raised my hand to any lady, but by this stage, my verbal abuse could be horrific.

When it was all over, I will never forget what happened. I went inside and Daddy was waiting. All he said was, "Son, it is all right to get pissed off and give these young girls a little hell every now and then, but you went too far."

His words were more painful than any whipping I ever experienced. They immediately went down to the inner parts of my soul, as the irony was not lost on me in that moment. The man who had been unmercifully mean and cruel to my mother for decades had just told me that I was too mean and cruel to a young lady. The cycle is vicious: shame, then anger, followed by drunkenness, which leads to horrific actions that need to be medicated. Rinse, wash, repeat. I wallowed in the cycle for seven long years before stopping it dead in its tracks through the power of the Gospel. It is hard for me to write about it to this very day.

Chief in front of his work truck in the mill village

*Hunter, Chief and Me in our den during a drinking binge from
the dark days*

CHAPTER 8

ADDICTION OF THE SON

G oing into ninth grade I was still near the bottom of the
social circles at school. I was lacking confidence and trying
to find my way. I had one friend who used to take me out to shop-
lift and vandalize. He was an amazing shoplifter and taught me to
steal a wide variety of things I didn't really need, from sunglasses
to candy bars to clothes. He actually stole a fishing rod once by
running it from his neck down to his feet under his clothes. He
had nerves of steel. His most lucrative heist was when he somehow
stole a full ring of keys that would open the old Coca-Cola vending machines. That meant he could stop at a vending machine at
any time and get all of the money out of it.

At the time, it wasn't really about the things being stolen, it
was about the adrenaline rush that came with stealing them and
the feeling of being on a team. You had to walk into the store in

an unassuming manner, keeping your eyes on the store clerk as she kept her eyes on you. Then you had to find the right amount of cover to subtly slide the goods in a pocket or in your pants while your buddy asked random questions as a distraction to the clerk. Finally, you had to pick up something inexpensive, like a pack of gum, and go to the front to pay for it with your heart about to beat out of your chest, wondering if she saw you take the stolen items. Once safely outside, you would celebrate like players who had just won a competition. For many, this just doesn't make sense, but for poor boys with very little to grab our attention, it was the ultimate competition.

We looked for this kind of rush everywhere. We spent plenty of time throwing eggs from our car at other cars passing us in the opposite direction, spotlighting couples who were "parking" in various places, and smashing mailboxes with baseball bats. Just normal mischief in small mill towns. Looking back, it was as if we were playing a sport. Often, we would get chased by a car we egged or a couple we had interrupted with the spotlight, which really brought the adrenaline. As soon as we were ahead of them any distance, we would kill the car lights and drive in the pitch black to try and get them off of our tail because we knew if they were chasing two guys in another car, they either had a gun or they were not scared to fight one-on-two, neither of which is a good sign. Once we were far enough ahead with no lights on, we would skid into a driveway and duck down to let the pursuer pass us by, hoping against hope that they didn't see us skid into the driveway. Fortunately, they never did, so the adrenaline rush would fill us with laughter and high fives as we moved on to the next victim.

During my sophomore year, I made the baseball team and gained a little more status. I also landed a steady girlfriend, which pushed me up even higher on the social ladder I so desperately wanted to climb. The combination of these two things, along with the newfound ability to drink six to eight beers each night, pushed me right into the mainstream. After being somewhat insecure and shy during middle school, I finally discovered that I had an alter ego that was funny, boisterous, and likable, especially when I was drinking. I used this to begin to make friends everywhere I went on the weekends. As a matter of fact, I can distinctly remember leaving my house on Friday and Saturday nights and thinking to myself just how lucky I was to have finally made it to the top of the social pecking order.

In order to add to some street cred to this newfound position, I got into a few fights after drinking just enough liquid courage to take the first swing. My first good one was with a guy who had cheated with my girlfriend when she was on a trip to Florida. His nickname was Dentals. I found him one evening at a baseball game and we got into a verbal sparring match. If I remember correctly, he denied it all. I talked down to him with threats and walked away feeling superior. That is where I should have stopped and declared a moral victory, but I never was one to be content with moral victories.

A few weeks later I loaded up with even more liquid courage, along with a carload of real street fighters: Muscles, Duck, and Pollard. We went out to settle the score and were driving around blaring the newly released Rocky anthem, ready to find Dentals. Unfortunately, by the time we found him I was pretty drunk, but not too drunk to hit him with all I had after we squared off in a bank parking lot. When it was all over, someone had kicked out the storefront glass to the bank and an alarm was going off very loudly. Everyone had to jump in the cars and scatter. Somehow we got away with it all and didn't go to jail that night, but I did come out of it with a nice six-stitch cut under one of my eyes and some road rash from the asphalt-wrestling. We hung out for several hours after the fight and reminisced about the actual sixty seconds of action, letting the story grow larger and larger as the night went longer.

I will never forget the reception I received when I finally went home. Daddy greeted me on the way in and had to know I was pretty drunk. He had me sit on our kitchen table, along with Muscles, so he could look at my eye. He checked it out and said it probably needed a few stitches while asking for a play-by-play of the fight itself, which was an absolute right of passage in the mill village. After giving Daddy the details, colored in our favor, I am sure, we prepared to go to the hospital to get sewn up.

As I was sitting there that night half drunk with a busted eye, I distinctly remember Daddy laughing at one point and saying, "I have been waiting so long for someone to shut that smartass mouth of yours!" I didn't take offense. He was right. My mouth had far outgrown my fists at that point and only a really solid right hook was able to convince me of that reality. In fact, I was going to need a few more left and right hooks to fully learn that lesson. But Daddy, who was a veteran of a dozen or more really good bare-knuckle street fights, was seemingly proud of my ambition and was hoping I would gain a little humility and a better left cross from the experience. I didn't gain either.

By the time I reached my junior year, I had found my place. I was fully accepted by the "in crowd" and was having a great time. School was very easy, so easy in fact that I found all kinds of ways to cheat and help my friends. In one class we developed a system of cheating so precise that when the tests were graded the teacher knew I had provided answers to several friends. I did so by writing all of my answers on a small piece of paper and sneezing loudly just as I threw it back over my shoulder to Bullet, who was sitting a few desks away in the rear. When our teacher saw that our tests were basically the same, she called Bullet out in the hall and said to him, "I know that Hot Dog helped you on this test, I just don't know how and you are going to tell me!" Fortunately, Bullet held strong with a shrug of the shoulders and a constant refrain of "I don't know what you are talking about. I studied hard for this test and did it myself." She had to be very frustrated. I am glad we didn't have cameras in the classrooms at that time.

Another time we got into serious trouble was the Friday night that my friends and I wound up at Sonic to use the restroom. It was a slow night with no adrenaline, and while we were in the restroom one of us decided to karate kick the mirror, which exploded all over the floor. That was funny to all, so on the way out another person (nameless to protect the guilty) grabbed one of the phones they used for ordering at the booths and yanked it out of the wall, bringing it into the car. We rode off laughing and playing the scene back, over and over.

On Monday, I was in class and our assistant principal, Ben Pillitary, came to get me and told me that two police detectives were there to question me. I remember him asking, "What did you do, son? How bad is it?" He knew it could be bad—drugs, theft, violence. Fortunately, it was just the fact that another Emma Sansom student was working at Sonic that night and saw us walk out right before they discovered the vandalism. It was very easy for him to identify all four of us. Just like in the movies, they brought us in one by one and told us they had us dead to rights and wanted to know exactly who broke the mirror and who tore the telephone receiver out of the wall. I had driven the "getaway car" so they threatened to hang it all on me if I didn't give up the names of the perpetrators. That is the day I learned thieves, crooks and vandals don't have friends. Each and every one of us sang like canaries and gave them the names of the two vandals among us as soon as they questioned us with their guns on their sides. As I recall, I think all that was required was monetary restitution, as Sonic decided to go easy on us.

These and many more were the stories of theft, vandalism, street fights, and all manner of mischief in the mill village. If there were time, I could write about the race riot where bricks and clubs were used to bust up cars and faces. I could talk about a high school friend literally punching through a car windshield with his bare fist just to intimidate the folks inside and let them know that this was a white hangout spot and blacks were not allowed. I could walk you through the story of a student's father taking a pitch fork type hoe and burying it an inch or more into the leg of one of my friends who had come on his property to fight his son, teaching him the enduring lesson that a man's home is indeed his castle. There were also more tame stories of drag races on country roads and city highways, along with untold damage to public property just for the rush of getting away with it. Pent-up energy from boys in small towns is a very dangerous thing, but the cure for it is restitution, not incarceration. As an example, one friend was caught teeing off on a mailbox with a baseball bat from a truck bed, a regular staple of late night fun, and had to go to that house and install a new one at his own expense under the supervision of the angry owner after being identified as the perpetrator. That cured him from that activity from that point forward.

❧ • ☙

During these crazy high school years, home didn't change much so I spent a lot of my time anywhere but there. Daddy wasn't drinking as hard or as long as he did in our younger years, and my parents weren't fighting with the same vigor, but they still had real conflicts. The source of tenuous peace was my mother's understandable resignation. In many ways, she had lost the will to fight. She had fallen into a deep depression when I was in eighth grade. Mother's depression was the kind that would keep her in bed for most of the day more days than not. Over time, it began to affect her ability to do basic things, like driving, reading, or writing a check.

Daddy was out hustling business and playing golf, as he was having some real success for the first time. He was not spending nearly as much time at Fred and Jean's Lounge or the Moose Lodge, but he was still a man who had to have two to three ladies in his life at all times. This was his Achilles' heel throughout his life. He and Mother had begun to live very separate lives in our small home, and it made the air thick with tension. Mother became isolated and only had joy when she would go out to her parents' house in Hollypond. Hunter and I no longer wanted to visit there for long stretches and she rarely went alone, so she became more and more bound to our home, fighting a crippling depression with drugs like Adavan.

Mother's depression brought a tangible feeling of gloom over our entire house, and this made me want to get out as much as possible. Not because I wasn't willing to help her, but as a self-centered sixteen-year-old I had no idea what to do. The days of physical violence were past, as Daddy probably intuitively knew that Hunter and I were now big enough to stop it. Moreover, Mother was very skinny and pitiful by this time, so it would have been unconscionable. The last time he laid a hand on her that I remember was when I was fourteen years old. Hunter had been out drinking the night before as a sixteen-year-old and had been caught by the police. Daddy had to go get him out of jail that morning and he was livid. He brought Hunter home and immediately put him in the backyard raking leaves, wanting him to work all day. I think Daddy and Hunter had some type of argument and Daddy pulled off his leather belt, as he had often done when we were smaller. Mother jumped in the middle of them and startled yelling at Daddy, "H.M., don't you hurt him!" She had seen Daddy's temper and she had seen him fight grown men, so she was worried about where this was going. Daddy drew back and hit Mother on her leg with his belt. I didn't see the hit, but I heard it and I saw the exact belt print bruise on Mother's leg for a week or more. She was a protector and she was willing to take our whippings for us, which she did more than once, but this was the last time.

In 1987, I reached my senior year and was looking ahead to graduation. One thing I always had going for me was a good brain so I could make good grades with very little effort. I rarely studied in high school and still managed to stay in the top of my class. I was coming out of high school with my sights set on college, specifically Auburn University. Jason and I wanted to go there together and probably would have if he had not died in that tragic accident. Following Jason's accident, I had no desire to go off to college and decided to stay at home and go to our local junior college, Gadsden State Junior College, or "Harvard on the Hill," as we called it.

I finished two semesters there while spiraling deeper and deeper into addiction and depression. I was still making good grades, but most of my life was spent working for Daddy or drinking with friends. It was during this period that I had that tragic automobile accident. The darkness of the time is still vivid for me even now, as I was stuck in the rut that had captured so many Carnes in the previous two generations. I was now following in their footsteps - I was squandering my God-given potential in life.

It was at this exact time I was given a great gift I will never forget. The first time I returned to calculus class after the accident, my professor spoke what I can only call a supernatural word of knowledge over me. It would not come to fruition for another three years, but she spoke it that day to a broken, confused young man. She'd asked me to come to her office after class, and said she had read about my recent automobile accident and knew about Jason's death just a few months earlier. Now mind you, at this time I presented myself in a posture of absolute rebellion against society. I had really long hair and an earring, which are not a big deal today, but they were at that time in Gadsden. I also had a really poor reputation. Yet this dear saint either saw something different in me or was told something by God. However it happened, she was able to see beyond all the externals.

As we sat in her office, she told me a story about her brother being killed at about the age of eighteen. He had a best friend who struggled mightily with this death and endured a great season of trials as well. At some point after that difficult season, he had managed to turn it all around for good and God had begun to use him to lead and encourage others. She then told me that often God puts us through difficult trials in life because He wants to use us in special ways later. She then spoke the word of knowledge by saying that she firmly believed all the tragedies currently happening in my life were simply a time of preparation for God to use me in a special way in this life. As she said these words, I had enough fear of God to be reverent and hear her out. I sat there with tears running down my cheeks, not uttering a word. At the end she prayed for me. As I rose to walk out of her office, I remember thinking to myself, "Lady, you've got the wrong guy. If you only knew what a messed-up and corrupt life I am leading *right now* you would never say things like that about me."

But if the Lord wants to make a crooked stick straight, who can stop Him? If He takes a vessel of dishonor and makes it honorable, not even the vessel can resist His will. Service to God was nowhere on my radar. I had contemplated that back at the graveyard when I was a pallbearer for Jason, and I had walked away from it for the so called "good life." This professor, though, knew something I didn't. She saw something in me I certainly couldn't see in myself, nor did anyone else see it other than my mother. She somehow knew that the absolutely hellish six months I had just endured was going to be a foundation for a position of spiritual leadership in just a few years. I had no clue. Several years later I wrote her a card, reminding her of this moment and how her prophecy had been fulfilled. I told her just how far away from God I'd been at the very time she was telling me that God was real and was going to use me greatly because of all this pain. She told me she knew just how far I was from God at that time, but she could see a different future for me. It was surreal then; it is even more so now.

After this junior college year, one of my best friends, Mike Nelson, aka "Bullet," had a connection through his mom with a guy that worked for Disney World and he needed a riding mate to go with him and work there for the summer as well. I knew almost nothing about it, but it was a lifeguarding job and it sounded cool, so I volunteered. In order to go to Disney and lifeguard, the first thing we had to do was get a lifeguarding certification. Fortunately, we had a friend who had that baseline certification and after a few hours in a residential pool, she very graciously signed off on our abilities. The next hurdle was the real lifeguarding week of training at Disney; and the instructors here were not our friends, nor did they sign off so easily. I almost drowned multiple times during the training process. I think we had to tread water with legs only holding a ten-pound brick for ten minutes, dive down eighteen feet to get a scuba diver off the bottom of the pool, and swim five-hundred meters in ten minutes or less. I was not that strong of a swimmer, but somehow I made it out alive.

After passing all the swim tests, you had to pass an eye exam as well. My vision is about 20/200 uncorrected, so I didn't have a chance. But much like Chief, I was always adept at finding a way to beat almost any system. In this instance, I simply faded to the back of the line while everyone in front of me read the exact same 20/20 line at the bottom with no problem. That line was only about eight letters long, so I just memorized it. When I stood up to the line to spout off the letters, I could barely see the extra-large single letter at the top, but I dutifully recited the 20/20 letters from memory and was pushed on through. This summer at Disney is where I was introduced to psychedelic mushrooms by Murph, a guy I met from upstate New York. Murph had put everything he owned on his back and rode his brand new Kawasaki Ninja down to Disney for this job. He was a great guy and it didn't take him long to find the local drug dealers. He and others were the very first people I ever met that were not from Alabama, except for my cousins from Flint, Michigan, as we never really traveled anywhere outside of Alabama when I was growing up. That is one thing about living in working-class families in small towns: your world gets very small because you rarely leave the place where you were born.

I certainly had a lot of fun during this summer and met many interesting people from all over the US. As was our custom, Bullet and I dutifully gave many of them nicknames. There was "Bobby Knight" from Massachusetts, who used to like to coach everyone when we were playing pick-up basketball. "Stevo," the quiet guy from New York and maybe the only one who didn't do drugs. "Jimbo," the black belt from the Midwest somewhere who was older and more mature than most, and "Fast Freddy," who mostly kept to himself. Looking back, I can only imagine how country "Bullet" and "Hot Dog" were to these guys when we came rolling into town in Bullet's 4Runner with accents so thick they could barely understand what we were saying. In fact, when I was teaching guests how to drive the small Sea Sprite boats at the Contemporary Resort where we worked, they would constantly beg me to keep speaking, as though I were some type of circus animal they had never known existed. It garnered lots of attention and I had fun with it, but it was truly shocking to these folks to hear an Alabama accent as thick as mine. It was the first time in my life I realized I had an accent. To be honest, I never could appreciate just how thick our accent was until I had been away from Gadsden for several decades and came back to hear my nieces talk as young children, when the accent is at its peak.

After this summer in Disney World, I was off to the University of Alabama with my childhood friend, Craig "Goose" McGriff. At the university, I would have two more years of deeper and deeper addiction before the words of my calculus professor would spring forth in my life and this multigenerational root of addiction would be dug up and laid bare to die. That is when the seed of the Gospel of Jesus finally germinated in my life and changed everything.

Just a few weeks after Jason's death when I was spiraling downward

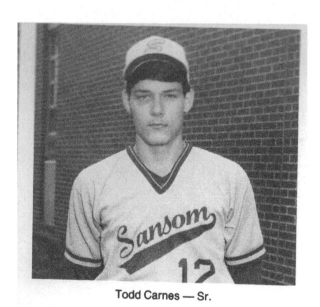

Todd Carnes — Sr.

Senior in High School

PART TWO:

NEW LIFE – NEW CALLING

"Here is a trustworthy saying that deserves full acceptance: Christ Jesus came into the world to save sinners – of whom I am the worst. But for that reason I was shown mercy so that in me, the worst of sinners, Christ Jesus might display his immense patience as an example for those who would believe in him and receive eternal life.

The Apostle Paul, *I Timothy 1:15—16*

CHAPTER 9

ADDICTION'S ANTIDOTE

Everybody liked Goose because he was a phenomenal athlete and he wasn't scared of anything. He also often stood on the outskirts of much that happened in the mill village because Goose was one of only two guys in my high school friend group who had real faith and a moral compass. Having a moral compass while relating to a large group of rowdy guys focused on sexual exploits and drunken binges is a tough thing to do, but Goose pulled it off most of the time. He never would have been able to do this if he hadn't earned respect from the other guys, both on the athletic fields and in fights when necessary. So the combination of his athletic abilities and his unique confidence in who he was, regardless of peer approval, actually gained him peer approval. Ironic for sure, but that is usually how it works.

One day he called and said he was going to the University

of Alabama next year and heard I might be interested in going as well. He asked if I would want to room with him. I was in such a chaotic spiral that I don't think I even had a plan for what was next, so his call and invitation to room together actually formulated a plan for me. This decision would be one of the most transformational choices of my life.

I landed in Tuscaloosa with Goose in a single bedroom apartment just off campus, as we couldn't afford the two-bedroom option. This first year I spent partying hard on campus, primarily with Goose's brother, Chub, and other friends from Gadsden who were at the university. Goose was aggravated with us most of the time, but he has the patience of Job so he tolerated the chaos that first year, often with 4-6 people from Gadsden crashing our apartment for the weekend. Soon he had branched out and become friends with some guys from a campus ministry organization, Campus Crusade for Christ, and began to relate to some other guys like himself, normal jock types who also had faith and a moral compass. He had never really experienced anything like this before. With this newfound support from other believers, his faith life began to blossom and he became more and more committed. I, on the other hand, went further and further down a path of addiction and destruction. The payment for my lifestyle became more and more costly, while Goose's rewards for a godly lifestyle paid higher and higher dividends.

At this point I began to drink to the point of blacking out, and this was the case most every weekend. After playing with alcohol for a few years and using it to help me climb the social ladder, it now had its hooks in me and I couldn't do anything about it. For several years, I was drinking heavily two or three times a week and most of those nights I would wake up the next morning, sometimes in places I didn't even recognize, and not have any rec-ollection of what had happened. Once I woke up with a torn and bloody shirt only to find out that I had been in a fight with several guys. I had to ask who they were and why we'd been fighting.

There were other times I woke up with bloody and swollen knuckles and assumed I had fought, but would later find out I was just violently mad at some point and had pounded on a wall or a car. Another time, I awoke all stitched up from a fight I could barely remember. I was a twenty-year-old man who had this pent-up and unprocessed rage from the bad cards I had been dealt. My childhood had taught me that things that are shameful should never be admitted or discussed for any reason. I would hide these things and this rage while I was sober, but once enough alcohol or pot got into my system, my normal filters came off.

At that point, all my emotions channeled directly into anger, which poured out onto strangers and friends alike. The old proph-ecy of Chief had come to fruition in my life.

During this time I caused tremendous pain for myself and others. I distinctly remember what it was like to be held captive by alcohol. Almost every night when I went out drinking, which was most every Thursday through Saturday, I would say over and over to myself, "Just chill out tonight and only drink a six pack ... don't get carried away, that just leads to problems." I don't think it ever happened. Every single time I said this to myself, I always bought just a six pack of Coors Light and when I finished, I either bought another six pack or I went out to the clubs and started drinking liquor until I blacked out. It is a horrible way to live. You drink all weekend and cause all kinds of problems, then you muddle through to Wednesday only to do it all again. What is even worse, you have now become the type of person you hated as a child.

Goose was a great friend during this time and he went far above and beyond where he probably should have gone. In fact, multiple leaders within Campus Crusade were telling him that he should move out of our apartment to go live with some sane, sober students who would build him up rather than living in the hellish party place we called home. I would have given him the exact same advice, but Goose is unique. He is loyal to a fault. I was his friend and he was loyal to me, even though he often wanted to strangle me. Somehow he resisted the calls to do what seemed best for him and stayed with me for three more years at school, two of which were filled with drunken debauchery. One great thing he did during this time is he would find just the right times to speak a very straight, honest, prophetic word into my life. It would always make me uncomfortable when it happened, but I couldn't get mad because I knew it was true and I knew his motivation.

For example, one day we were riding around and he just said out of the blue, "Todd, when do you think you will stop drinking? We both grew up with dads that were alcoholics and that was hellish for us. I know you don't want to repeat that for your kids, so when exactly do you think you can put the bottle down and quit drinking? Do you ever think about that?"

"To be honest, Goose, I haven't really thought about it."

"Well you should give it some thought because I don't think our dads ever thought they would do all the things they did as husbands and fathers and I don't think you can lay it down and quit even now, much less in several more years."

Other times, he would get a little more angry with me and once he even told me, "You are just a whore, man, that is what you are, you're a whore!" Strong words, but he had a right to say them. As I recall, he said all of those things in year one, and he still had to survive year two with me in this condition!

That second year at Alabama was even darker and crazier. This is the year I went to a James Taylor concert at the amphitheater in Birmingham and don't remember driving the forty-five minutes back to Tuscaloosa. It was the year I was at my girlfriend's house late at night and her ex-boyfriend, Doug, showed up. As I remember, he walked right into her house at about one a.m. He and I started shoving and yelling and she got in between us as we were heading outside. Her dad woke up, came to the living room, and told Doug he had to leave. He refused at first and it was total chaos among the four of us. Her dad was trying to keep this fight from going down in his living room, so he put his arm around Doug and was walking him out the front door. After a few minutes, her dad came back inside and told me, "Hot Dog, you've got to go. Doug is outside and he has a gun and he put it to his head and is threatening to kill himself if you don't leave." At that point, no rational person would walk outside knowing Doug had a gun that he had already pointed toward his own head. Unfortunately, I was neither sober nor rational, or didn't realize I had a choice, so I walked right outside. Doug jumped out of his car immediately, fortunately without the pistol, and the fight started. Kate's dad had managed to get us out of the house, but he had two really nice Cadillacs in his driveway and we rolled across the top of one of them before landing on the concrete, swinging haymakers at each other. Both of us were a little drunk so although many punches were thrown, very few landed and no extreme damage was done to anything other than the Cadillac. Kate's dad bravely came back outside and eventually got us separated and threatened to call the police, or maybe he already had. Either way, we both got in our cars and left. Crisis averted.

The final straw of this season of life came when we threw a keg party at our house. Goose knew what was coming all weekend, so he left to go and stay with his newfound friends. It was during this weekend that I started drinking liquor really early in the evening and wound up in a fight with one of my best friends, Bullet. I don't really remember how or why it happened, but I took a nasty left to the eye and got a cut that had to be stitched up. Two other friends also got in a fight with a similar result, multiple stitches to the eye of another. Goose came home and surveyed all the damage and was livid. He sat down and wrote me a letter I still have to this day. Here are some excerpts:

> *As I reflect back on last night I see a place where Satan was working hard and he was pleased with what happened last night, not with just you and Mike but with everything that was going on here. My heart is filled with hurt because I love all of you so much. It hurts to see how you all give in to alcohol and how you let it affect your lives. Have you ever seen any good results from drugs and alcohol? There is a lot more to life! Todd, I am sharing this with you because of how much you and our friendship means to me. I have been on both sides and believe me the side where God is first in my life is the best thing I have ever experienced. . . . Todd, God's love and grace is sufficient and can take away the hurt and anger you feel right now. God loves you and offers a wonderful plan for your life and Satan hates you and offers a terrible plan for your life.*
>
> *A Friend who Cares, Craig "Goose" McGriff*

When I read it, shame pulsed throughout my entire body. It

would be another six to eight months before I would come to faith and settle down, but I kept the letter. That spring I hung out with a few of Goose's Christian friends and they were not too weird, some were actually pretty cool. I think I even attended a Bible study he was leading a few times, but summer came and Goose went home to work. I had secured a job lifeguarding at a local country club so I stayed in Tuscaloosa and continued to wallow in the mud of drunkenness and debauchery. I also stayed in Tuscaloosa because my grades that spring were three Fs, one D, and one B. I was generally a straight-A student with just a little effort, but I had lost all touch with reality that spring. I was depressed, didn't really care to be in school, and wasn't sure why I was even at the university, so I basically stopped going to class. I didn't even take two of my final exams because I was so far behind it seemed useless. I failed Fluid Dynamics and Strength of Materials. When Chief saw those grades, he very clearly told me that I had one mulligan in which to make those kinds of grades and I had just played it, so if I ever did that again he was done providing for my education. I knew he was serious and never let that happen again.

Just before spring semester ended that year, something happened to me that had never happened before. A black man came into my house. It was shocking to me. It even angered me. In the mill village, this was a line you didn't cross. We had picked up black guys from the housing projects and taken them to soccer practice and had great times on the field, but I had never been in their homes, nor had they been in mine. Geraldine, the maid, had been in my house when she was doing work, but not as an invited guest. I had been in the homes of the black people when I was working on their house, but again, not as an invited guest. As a matter of fact, there was a single black kid that went to our elementary school and he was a good friend. I wanted to invite him over to my house one afternoon and I could not. His name was Kevin and his dad was an engineer at the Goodyear factory in our town, so they were a very affluent family, much more so than us. When I asked my mother about this, she explained to me that he couldn't come over because of the uproar it would cause in our neighborhood. She was actually apologetic about it. Once she brought it up, I understood fully what she was saying even as a 4th grader, as the derogatory N-word was used very casually in my neighborhood. As a matter of fact, when we chose sides for pick-up teams almost every day and chanted the famous rhyme, "Eenie, meenie, miney, moe, catch a tiger by his toe, if he hollers make him pay . . . ," we never used the word *tiger* in that rhyme. We always inserted the N-word for tiger. I never heard the rhyme any other way until I was an adult. That is how commonly it was used in the all-white working-class neighborhoods of the mill village. Even worse, I could have a friend at school who was black and yet use the N-word very casually and never even realize that these two things were in such contradiction.

So the day Goose brought home his African American friend, Beau, I was stunned to see him in my house. I don't think I ever said anything to Goose, but I certainly felt like he had crossed a line. I didn't even consciously know it was a line, but when I saw it being crossed it just felt wrong. I had a visceral reaction to it—not something premeditated, purely visceral. Over the next few months, I actually started getting to know Beau as we played tennis together and some basketball as well. As we hung out, I became more and more comfortable around him and soon it didn't feel so odd when he was at our house. I would be lying, however, if I said it was instantaneous. Deep-seated belief systems engrained in childhood do not change overnight. It takes time and effort to identify them, as they live at the subconscious level. This incident of Beau walking into my house in college was the catalyst that totally changed my entire belief system in regard to race. The best part of this story is Beau became my roommate a year and a half later, and eventually served as a groomsman at my wedding. This proves the point that it just takes one authentic friendship with someone of another race to break through deeply held racial barriers. Over the next few years Beau and I were great friends and as a result, Beau worked to overcome racial stereotypes about whites in his family while I was overcoming stereotypes about blacks in mine.

After a summer of lifeguarding at the local country club, I settled into school again for the fall football season, but this would be my last party season. Though I didn't know it was coming, this was to be the season of rebirth. Late August and September were spent as usual in class and party mode in the run-up to September 28, 1991. This was a special date because it was the day I was going to turn twenty-one. I could finally do away with all of my fake IDs and get in any club at any time without the anxiety of them realizing my ID was really the military ID of my childhood friend Troy.

September 28th of that year was on a Friday, so in reality I turned 21 at 12:01 a.m. on Thursday night. That meant me and the crew could hit the clubs hard starting just after midnight. We partied in Tuscaloosa Thursday and Friday, then drove to Auburn, Alabama, to watch a football game on Saturday and go to the infamous Supper Club on Saturday night with friends. After this three-day binge, I dragged myself home to Tuscaloosa sometime on Sunday and was as dead as you might imagine. As I was lying there on our couch hungover and feeling horrible, I was really depressed. What was so depressing was the fact that this type of partying was the highest pinnacle of my life and I had reveled in it for the last seventy-two hours across the entire southern part of our state with a bunch of good friends, yet I was empty. The music had stopped, and everybody was home and I was depressed and alone. All of this made me acutely aware that my life was absolutely miserable if this was all that I valued. It is like eating something until you throw up and then you never want to eat that particular food again. I was honest with myself and realized it was all fake and empty. *Surely there has to be more to life than this?* I thought.

I was in this state of mind when Goose bounced in with his usual energy and said, "Hey man, you going to that Bible study I told you about with Bard Johnston tonight?"

"No way, I feel like hell, bro, can't make it. Maybe next week."

"Come on, man, this is the first one and if you miss this one it will be hard to know the guys and actually participate. Come on, get up and get your butt over there." Then he literally slapped a Bible in my hand and pushed me out the door. Nothing in me wanted to go to this Bible study, but I felt obligated to Goose and he was pushing hard. Also, I had met Bard playing pick-up basketball and he seemed like a normal guy, so I thought to myself, *I will go one time and if it is weird, I'm not going back.*

I drove over to the clubhouse at Bard's apartment complex and there were about seven guys there including Bard. I just wanted to get this over with quickly so I could get home and get some sleep. Bard started off with some type of introduction mixer and then handed out a small booklet he said we would cover this semester. After that, he very plainly explained the Gospel of Jesus

Christ. I don't remember his exact words, but he was very clear that you did not have to clean yourself up in order to give your life to Christ and become a Christian. He said that would be like trying to clean yourself up before you got into the shower. The Gospel was the good news, and that you can come to Jesus while you are filthy and He will clean you up. I had never heard this before. Someone had probably said it to me, but it is one thing for someone to say it but altogether different when you have ears that can actually hear it.

I said very little that night and listened, but the entire time I was thinking to myself, *Is this really true? I am sitting here filthy, hungover, wallowing in every evil thing, so is it really possible that I could give my life to Jesus in this condition? Surely I have to clean myself up for a season first, quit living like hell and learn to live clean. Then I can give my life to Him.* Bard, however, was saying that was foolish thinking. He was saying I should come to Jesus just as I was at that moment in my life. It was the perfect day for me to hear this message because I felt as empty and dirty as I had ever felt, and here was a guy saying that Jesus would cleanse me free of charge and He would do it right now if I would ask. I took the book and went home, saying very little to anyone.

Nobody likes tragedy, myself included, but it is usually in the midst of tragedy that we are awakened to the things that really matter in life. The first time I truly contemplated giving myself to Jesus I was ten years old and it was in the midst of a personal tragedy. In spite of the chaos that was in my home, I had some really good times at my elementary school, the Episcopal Day School. I wound up at this private school because the public schools in Gadsden were only integrated in 1972 and I was starting school in 1974. Knowing the racial dynamics of Gadsden in general, I have to assume it was a very tense time for everyone, so my parents somehow found to a way to get me into the Episcopal Day School where all the students were white. Most of the other students were from upper-middle-class families and lived much differently than us. The beautiful thing about elementary school at that time was kids didn't start their "classism" until middle school, so even a kid like me with older clothes that generally wreaked of cigarette smoke was not judged by those things, at least not overtly. That was special.

As a student, I was generally ranked toward the top of my class academically and I was near the top of the class athletically. I had so much fun during PE with Mrs. Faye Housley. We played kickball and capture the flag, ran races, and went on the best field trips ever. She took us to this cabin area in the woods regularly where we could fish and walk trails and look for snakes and scorpions. Once, one of my classmates tried to pet a snake, and it turned out as you would imagine. Bitten by a copperhead and off to the hospital. I learned how to swim at the pool near this cabin, and even though I almost drowned trying to swim a full lap by myself—ironic for someone who would later become a lifeguard—Mrs. Housley saved me at the last minute.

At this time, as has often been the case in my life, tragedy struck just as things were beginning to go well. As the fastest person in my third grade class and one of the better athletes, I would try to show off.

One day I was jumping toward some type of rolled-up mat and was going to land on my bent knees and spring off back to my feet. Somehow, I went all the way over the mat on my jump and hit square on the tiled floor. The next day my knee was swollen, which wasn't of grave concern given that I had smashed it against a tile floor. Unfortunately, this was not a simple injury that would clear up in a week or so. This was going to be a new, painful normal for me for the rest of my life. After my knee failed to return to normal, doctors became concerned and started running tests trying to figure out what was wrong. Meanwhile, my other knee decided to swell up as well.

After at least one stay in the hospital and several trips to Children's Hospital in Birmingham (ironically, the same place Chief was treated for his teenage tragedy), I was diagnosed with Juvenile Rheumatoid Arthritis (JRA). This was going to be a nemesis in my life, but it was especially painful to me at this time because of the devastating impact it had on my athletics, just like Chief's injury had on him. Modern medicine didn't really understand JRA in the 1970s, so the years ahead were mainly spent taking up to twelve aspirin a day, waking up with painfully stiff and swollen knees such that I could barely walk, taking hot baths that were supposed to help but really didn't, and playing through the pain in soccer, baseball, basketball, and flag football. I excelled in these sports even with the constantly swollen and painful knees, but it was frustrating. The only remedy available was to have them drained and injected with steroids at Children's Hospital in Birmingham, which I often endured. This was the most painful medical experience of my childhood. I honestly don't think Novocain was injected before the draining took place. I was now the one yelling and screaming at Children's Hospital, just as Chief had heard the same from other children being "picked" during his stay there. It was so bad that once a friend and his mom traveled with us, and when I came out of the room, my friend was so upset he was crying and inconsolable after listening to my painful cries and yells.

This was a sustained season of loss for me as a child, and as a result, I began asking more serious questions about life, even as a ten-year-old. We had neighbors at the time, the Knight family, who went to a "health and wealth" prosperity church. They loved my family and we loved them, as they often had been the ones to come to our rescue when the cops came out to break up fights at our house. The father, Jerry, went through a radical conversion at some earlier point in life and had ended up at this congregation. That being the case, they were convinced that the laying on of hands and anointing with oil would cure me of this harsh disease ravaging my joints. At least twice, maybe more, I was taken to this church by my mom (Chief never went; he had disdain for this church in particular because of its health and wealth manipulation), where these neighbors would have pastors and others lay hands on me, praying in tongues and calling out loudly for my healing. As is usually the case, it was an emotionally charged event that never had any tangible result other than my mother crying and me being given false hope. My neighbors were great folks who loved me dearly, but health and wealth theology is both deceptive and dangerous. It does so much harm to the sick and the poor, the very ones it claims to help. It makes you feel as though your faith is broken if God doesn't heal you right away, heaping both guilt and shame right back on your shoulders, when it proclaims to provide freedom. The only ones who ever really prosper are the well-dressed preachers at the front collecting the offerings.

There was one good result that came out of this time of testing, however. It was the fact that my physical and emotional pain put me in a place of desperation that caused me to actually pull out an old King James Bible and begin to read. I had only been to church when I was taken there to be prayed over by my neighbors, but I had heard my neighbors talk repeatedly about the miracles of Jesus. This caused me to take out that King James Bible and read all the red-letter healings performed by Jesus. I was hoping that somehow reading through these miracles would cause Jesus to heal me. It didn't work, but it did begin to awaken my young soul to the concepts of God, eternity, and salvation. These are the very first memories I have of anything spiritual, and lesson one was you can't force God to make your problems go away. The Lord gives and the Lord takes away and He does so in His own time.

After three years of pain and trying to understand spiritual concepts, I eventually abandoned that pursuit out of frustration and insecurity. As a sixth grader, I entered General Forest Middle School, which was very different than the Episcopal Day School. Sixth grade boys generally love to curse and tell off-color jokes as their favorite pastime. Initially, I would never participate because of the fear of God I had gained from my reading of the Bible. However, my faith was not very strong and I was all alone in this pursuit of holiness, so eventually I gave in and sought acceptance over holiness. Thus, I began my climb of the social ladder, albeit with the fear of God and hell still very much in my young conscience.

In high school, I was blessed to receive a long remission from my JRA and played sports once again, including a lot of church league basketball. As a part of these teams, I was exposed to both Bible teaching and pot smoking. I played with a bunch of guys who taught me to smoke pot before practice and we would have Royal Ambassador Bible training after practice. A unique combination for sure, but that is the reality of it. We had good teams and went to state finals most years. When my team of fourteen-year-olds went to the state championships in Montgomery, Danny brought Everclear (190 proof grain alcohol) on the bus for all of us to drink. When I was fifteen, our team was undefeated again and went to Birmingham for the finals against a team from Hoover, Alabama. Multiple players on our team got so drunk the night before that they were throwing up the day of the game. As a result, we got schooled by a team that obviously stayed sober the previous night. Along with these defeats, I was spiritually defeated, and I abandoned the entire pursuit of God for several years.

When Jason died following my senior year in high school, I seriously contemplated what it would mean to leave behind my foolish lifestyle and give myself to Jesus for the second time. I came very close to making that decision at the time, but I simply couldn't envision leaving my party life behind to follow Jesus into the unknown. I envisioned the Christian life as something very dull and lonely so I was not going to give up my hard earned social status for that type of life.

‣ • ‣

So it was that I had considered but rejected a life of faith twice before in my life – once as a disease stricken ten-year-old boy and again as a troubled eighteen-year-old rebel at his best friend's graveside. But this night, as a twenty-one-year-old, something was different. After a hellish birthday weekend partying with friends followed by Bible study with Bard and his group, I realized I was desperate for something much more meaningful in life than the so-called good life. Bard's words left an impression on me and opened the door for me to understand that just maybe, I could be open to the kind of commitment necessary to follow Jesus, whatever that meant, even though I didn't know all that was involved.

The booklet I had been given that night by Bard was about

fifty pages long, and I read it all that night. When I was finished, there was a prayer on the back cover that the author said you should read and pray to God so that He would save you. I knew very little about praying, so I read the prayer and added to it, "God, I am going to really give this thing a try this time. I don't want to be one of those guys who 'gets religion' for a few months and then goes right back to my old sinful life." I had even done this myself that time I begged for forgiveness in the back seat of Chris Baswell's car thinking we were all going to die, and then forgot all about it when we had arrived home safely. "No, this time, if it is real, I want it and I am going to really try for two weeks to see if this works, as I have to give it a chance to work. No partying for two weeks and I'll go to this Bible study and let's see what happens."

For those first two weeks, I didn't tell a soul because I didn't want to be ashamed if I went right back to the clubs and my old lifestyle. I was an undercover believer during that time, but soon I couldn't hold it in any longer. I went home on either the second or third week and asked Mother if she wanted to go to church on Sunday. I am sure she bit her tongue when I asked, but she did not overtly react and she agreed to go with me.

The only place we knew to go was the health and wealth Pentecostal church that had tried to heal me of JRA so many times as a kid. It was also the church where I'd had my one and only counseling appointment after Jason's death, an appointment where the pastor told me I needed to bury Jason and move on with life. He was right about that at the time, though he later had to resign after accusations arose of illicit homosexual liaisons. Now Mother and I were here on a Sunday morning, sitting near the back of the church. I have no idea what was said, but when the service was over they always had an altar call, a time when the preacher invites any who have needs, who may want prayer or anyone who wants salvation or healing, to please step out and walk down the aisle to the altar to do business with God. This day, before I even knew what was happening, I was on my way down the aisle. It wasn't planned, it just happened. Given my notorious reputation in the mill village, many who were there that day knew who I was. As I approached the pastor, I told him I wanted to rededicate my life. This was the best terminology I had at the time and I didn't want to say I was coming to get saved because that would mean I was lost just a few minutes or days ago. To be lost, to be something other than a Christian, was a really shameful thing in my mind, and I was shame-averse.

As I arrived at the altar and tried to say these words, my neighbor Jerry came down front to meet me along with some other men. As I was trying to say I wanted to rededicate my life, these men knew I was a sinner far from God and they overpowered me and said, "No son, you are coming to get saved. You are here to get saved today, glory hallelujah, Little Todd is getting saved today." I can still hear it, actually. They started praying in tongues and such and I just let go. I realized it didn't matter what I thought or what they thought. I didn't care if they said *saved* or *rededicated*. I was there to publicly proclaim that on the night of my life when I felt the dirtiest and most empty, I had been shown the Gospel of mercy and had said yes to God. I was ready to publicly drive a stake in the ground and proclaim it.

Of course, Mother was in tears. I don't remember much after that until I started driving back to Tuscaloosa. I remember driving and thinking, "If I die on this trip, I am not going to hell, I am going to heaven." I had confidence in that simple fact for the very first time in my life. I had buried several friends in the last few years and knew tomorrow was not promised, so the supernatural peace and rest I felt in knowing I was finally forgiven was above and beyond anything I had ever experienced.

When a local hellion in the mill village got saved, it was always big news and word traveled fast. Goose knew before I even arrived back to Tuscaloosa. He was waiting on me and said he heard I did something at church. I told him about it with the only vocabulary I had for it at that time and he was excited, but didn't go overboard. I am sure he had some skepticism and rightfully so, but his years of planting and watering, tilling and rebuking were finally paying off, and it was just beginning. Soon I had told Bard and my new Bible Study group. I told my old girlfriend when she called and I told everyone that asked. Finally, one night at this large gathering of about three-hundred college students gathered together for a Campus Crusade meeting, I stood and publicly declared how thankful I was for my roommate, Goose. That through all the drunkenness and fights and chaos, he stuck with me, his Little League teammate. I had finally heard and understood the Gospel and believed. Goose is a tough dude, but he has a soft heart, so he had to leave the room because he was weeping.

Now it was done. I was committed to Christ, Christ was committed to me, and I had told the world, at least my little side of it. Life was now exciting in Tuscaloosa, and my salvation was big news in Gadsden. It was the pivotal point of my life that shaped every single decision going forward. It was the decision that saved me from a life of depressed Sundays, looking for love in all the wrong places and seeking joy in a bottle, pill or experience. God had broken the generational Carnes' curse of addiction in an instant as the result of a single, humble prayer, but I would have doubts for years to come.

The next two years of my life at the University of Alabama were phenomenal. I was always sober, I was living without regret, and I was making new friends every day. I remember the first date I had with a Christian girl. I had no idea how to act, what to do, or what was expected of me. It was two months after I had given my life to Christ and it was Iron Bowl weekend in Alabama. Alabama and Auburn were playing in Birmingham and my party buddies from Gadsden had rented some rooms and asked me to join them for the weekend blast. Goose, on the other hand, had asked me to go on a double date with him to a "party" at a church in Birmingham. I had no idea how you could have a party at a church? This was the first pivotal point for me as a new believer. I had to choose between a huge weekend party with all the boys or a date with a Christian girl at a church, whatever that meant. I chose correctly, even though it was very uncomfortable to choose the unknown over the known. From that point forward, I never looked back. I immersed myself in this new Christian community and began to grow in my faith while experiencing good, clean fun for the first time since I was twelve years old.

Soon after this faith experience, I went home to Gadsden for another weekend. At this time, Chief had left Mother because of his longstanding affair with another lady in our community. Mother had not forced him to leave, but he had left so that he and his girlfriend could see each other at will in his newly rented apartment, as she was married as well and they needed this outside space. This particular weekend Chief was drinking pretty heavily and mother was worried about him being really drunk and all alone in that apartment. Yes, you read that correctly. She was worried about him even though he had abandoned her for this other lady. As the peacemaker in the home, I agreed to go over to Chief's apartment and stay with him a few days to help him get sober. As I entered his apartment, he was not sloppy drunk but he was in the sad drunk stage. One of the first things he said to me was, "Come here, Asshole. Your mother told me you got saved last week. That's good, son, that's real good!" As he said these words there were tears pouring out of his eyes. I think he had me by my hands and he was in a robe, his clothing of choice when drinking at home. It was actually awkward, but I knew that he was proud of me and he knew that I was finally going to pull my life out of the downward spiral I had been experiencing for the last seven years.

When Chief went to bed that night, I was aggravated with him. I was pissed that he was living here in this apartment so he could sleep with this other lady indiscriminately. It was embarrassing since I knew her family pretty well and it was the town's worst-kept secret. As such, I had no patience for his sad drunk foolish talk and didn't intend to listen to it as an adult after more than a decade of being forced to tolerate it as a child. I was only there to make sure he got sober without falling down the stairs of his sparsely furnished new apartment, as the bedroom was upstairs and daddy was not stable when he was drinking because of his built-up shoe. When he fell asleep that night, I took his bottle of whiskey and poured it out in the sink. The following morning he asked me where his whiskey was and I told him I poured it out. Rage hit his face when I said it, but he literally clinched his teeth and smiled. I know he wanted to cuss, but he couldn't bring himself to curse and yell at his newly converted son who had come over to protect him from himself the night before. I knew right then that I would not pour out any more of his liquor, nor would I sleep over to keep him from falling down the steps because he was drunk.

Several months after this episode, Daddy was drunk again and somehow wound up at his mother's house in the mill village. He had obviously been drunk for multiple days. He was unshaven, his hair was unkempt, and he had on a simple undershirt which was stained with different foods. The kitchens of mill village homes are very small, so it was crowded with me, Daddy, Mother, Mama Zana, and Aunt Juanita all standing and sitting around the table. Aunt Juanita had called Mother and asked her to come over because Chief was both ornery and in bad shape, and they didn't think they could take care of him. I also think he was ready to come home after four or five months in that lonely apartment. As we entered, Juanita and Mother began to talk about what to do with Chief. Soon thereafter, I was astonished that Mother was just going to let him walk right back into our house, drunk and helpless. That is certainly not what I wanted at that time, but there she was, coming to his rescue once again and receiving him back as though nothing had happened. We loaded him up out the back door of Mama Zana's home since he was too impaired to make it down the front steps. When we arrived, we put him to bed, and he never went back to the apartment except to retrieve the new furniture he had purchased for it, to replace the old furniture in our home. Predictably, that was not the end of the affair, but it was the last time he left home.

These two events are indicative of how my relationship with Chief was about to change over the next few decades. Up to this point in life, I had managed to both love Chief and serve as Mother's protector as much as possible. Now, as a new believer, my zeal for honor and purity was about to spring forth and fracture my relationship with Chief for a season. During this time,

I traveled extensively on missionary journeys around the world, so our face-to-face time was limited. When we were together, we had tough conversations and real conflict as I sought to hold Chief accountable for the decades of emotional pain Mother had experienced, pain which had now left her chronically depressed. Our relationship would hit its lowest point during this period as I began to work through these traumatic issues in our family, a process that would ultimately require fifteen years.

Me with Beau and John Mantooth after college graduation

Celebrating a Tug of War victory on Waikiki Beach in Honolulu

CHAPTER 10

FIRST MISSIONARY JOURNEY

Following my first senior year at the University of Alabama (my two-Fs semester had set me back a year), I embarked on my first missionary journey. It was to Hawaii for the summer with Campus Crusade. I know, I know. Hawaii, right? It was tough. Sunny and seventy-eight degrees every single day living right off Waikiki Beach in Honolulu with about seventy other college students. The only struggle was cooking cheeseburgers all day at a Jack-in-the-Box restaurant in a polyester uniform, as we all had to get day jobs as a part of the mission.

I had been invited to be a part of this special summer project by the adult leadership of Campus Crusade at the University of Alabama, as they had seen me grow in my faith in an accelerated manner throughout my first year as a believer. As a result, they challenged me to go on this project and develop my faith. As participants in this summer project, our primary purpose was to learn and grow in our faith and to tell our faith stories to the international tourists gathered there throughout the year. This was some of the best times of my life as I developed deep relationships with so many people from around the nation. There was Kirby and Meredith from Texas Tech, Perry from UNC, Nelly from Louisiana Tech, Will and Dawn from LSU, five of us from 'Bama and many others. We each had to raise about $3,000 to go on this trip, and while for many this was a relatively easy task because they had the support of their home churches, I, on the other hand, did not have any real Christian connections from home, so it was quite a challenge for me. I remember my mother helping me along the way and somehow, God provided for me and it transformed my life in a million ways. That is why I never miss a chance to support young students who are taking on a project similar to this one. It can be a life-altering experience for them that translates into life altering experiences for hundreds or even thousands.

While I was in Hawaii, I learned how to date in an honorable way, to share my faith with total strangers, to study the Bible, and to pray. We lived on a high school school campus which was empty for the summer and slept on army cots, bathed in a locker room, and ate outdoors. I remember toward the end of the summer an adult Campus Crusade leader, Dale, pulled me aside and said he saw in me natural leadership ability and real commitment to the faith. No one had ever given me those kinds of compliments and I surely did not think of myself as a leader. I am not sure I even had a definition for leadership at that point in my life, and here he was saying he saw natural leadership in *me* and felt that I could lead others. He went on to say I would be a great candidate to join the staff of Campus Crusade and impact other college students who desperately need faith and direction, like I had one year prior.

It was encouraging, but to be honest my very first reaction was an internal voice that said, "Hey, Todd, this Christian thing has been really good for you and it is the path for you, but don't get carried away and let it take over your whole life. You are graduating with a civil engineering degree and you don't want to go out and beg for money to do ministry, so just keep doing what you are doing, but don't get too radical." With that voice going off in my mind, I promised Dale I would think about it and see what happened. It was my first invitation into ministry, and I was obviously not ready. I still needed more time to grow in the faith and time to sort out what was temporary and what was eternal. Even so, in retrospect, I went to Hawaii as an insecure follower trying to figure out my faith, and returned from there eight weeks later as a spiritual leader very confident in my faith.

After this summer project, I returned to campus for my fifth and final year of college. I was rooming in a house with seven other guys and we had a great time. Several of these guys really had an impact on my life, as they were thinkers and had been in the faith long enough to teach me a lot about the Bible. This allowed us to talk and think deeply about things that mattered. Throughout this year, I became a leader in the same Campus Crusade movement that had brought me to faith one year prior. As I gained confidence in my leadership, something I had always been lacking, I began to bring others in as well. As a testimony to the radical transformation God had worked in my life, once a guy named "Cub" Driggers was at a Crusade meeting and saw me up front leading. He told the guy he was with that I shouldn't be trusted because I was a wild and angry guy. He had seen me at parties at my worst, several times. My friend had to explain that I had come to faith within the last year and had totally changed.

It was a great year to tell my transformation story and I told it at large group meetings I organized in the school of engineering, at fraternity meetings, anywhere and everywhere I could get an audience. As that year was coming to a close, I began to see how I wanted to invest my life so I started making plans for a second missionary journey. This time it was going to be to Russia for one year, as it was 1992 and with the recent collapse of the Soviet Union, there was a window of opportunity that had not been possible for the last seventy years. I interviewed for a few engineering jobs early in the spring, but decided my calling was to work in ministry in Russia and stopped my search. This decision would launch me into twenty years of ministry work around the world, but there were going to be many detours and speed bumps along the way.

The very first detour was a tragic one. There was a leader in the Christian organization Athletes in Action named Wayne Waddell. He was working with the athletes at LSU, though he had roots in Alabama. He was organizing a team of college students to go to Russia for a one-year term and spread the Gospel and I had heard about this, though I don't remember how. I didn't know Wayne and he didn't know me, but he was very cavalier by reputation, as was I, so we were a perfect match. Our mutual friends connected us and told us we would get along just fine, so I had a few conversations with him over the phone and he decided it would be a good fit for me to join his team. We would go to Russia in September 1992, and work on a college campus for one year on a team of about ten others.

With that plan in place, I returned home to work in Chief's company as a carpenter for the summer while I raised funds and prepared to leave in the fall. Chief was truly disappointed to see me "throw away" my education and told me so, but he knew I was just as headstrong as him so he eventually backed off and accepted it. When I landed back at home, I found myself doing the same menial labor I was doing as an unskilled fifteen-year-old, though now I was twenty-three with a civil engineering degree. That made throwing trash on a pickup truck and bringing it to the fly infested landfill while working under the supervision of a local carpenter a very humbling experience. One day I was alone cleaning up a job we had finished when Chief came by to check on my progress. He said something about it being hot and hard work, and I remember telling him Jesus was a carpenter as well, so if it wasn't beneath him, it certainly wasn't beneath me. He went home and recounted this conversation to Mother, who later told me Daddy was shocked by my words, but I think he was also proud in some small way. He definitely wanted me to be a civil engineer and not a missionary, but if I was going to be a missionary he wanted me to be genuine in my faith. My hard word and humility during this very difficult season assured him that my faith was real. He never mentioned anything to me about this interaction, but it felt good to hear his words from Mother, as I know it had to be hard on Chief to pour all of that money and sacrifice into my education only to feel like I was throwing it away chasing some sort of naïve fantasy.

But in regard to the actual missionary journey to Russia, things started to fall apart in June in a very tragic way. Wayne, our team leader, had one of his daughter's suddenly diagnosed with Leukemia. This meant his family was immediately whisked away to a specialty cancer hospital and everything to do with the Russia mission had to be cast aside. Because I was to have been a supporting player on his team, this meant that the journey was canceled for me as well. In an instant, my post college plan vanished. My $7 an hour job cleaning up construction sites in the mill village, which was supposed to be a temporary way to raise money for my true calling, suddenly didn't seem as glamorous as designing subdivisions and roads for $30,000 annually. I was more than a little confused by the situation even as my heart went out to the Waddell family. Not long after this, Wayne's daughter died. That tragic event put him into a black hole spiritually and emotionally, as it would anyone. I reached out to him as best I could to be supportive but had no real idea how to respond to this type of tragedy as a twenty-three-year-old.

Interestingly, twenty-five years later, I was put into a spiritual black hole myself, and although I had not talked to Wayne in over two decades, I reached out to him to ask how he ever escaped that dark place. He was gracious and walked me through his process of anger, rage, depression, and restoration. When you find yourself in a six-foot ditch where it is cold, dark and damp, you always want to talk to someone who has been in a ten-foot ditch and escaped. That was Wayne for me and that is the beauty of the worldwide church, where all of us function as brothers and sisters to encourage one another in our most challenging seasons of life.

After these events, I found myself wondering what in the world I should do? I had forgone engineering interviews in the spring, so I had no opportunity there. As a blue collar family, we didn't have any connections in Gadsden who could help me find a position in engineering. What I did have was a young lady at the University of Alabama who had caught my attention about four months earlier. She was this beautiful volleyball player from Michigan, Kerri Kuiper. Even though I had wanted to date her now for six months or more, I had resisted taking this next step because I thought I was going to Russia and didn't want to start a relationship with her and then leave her in limbo. Now, however, I was sitting in Gadsden somewhat confused, but with Kerri Kuiper on my mind. I couldn't decide exactly what to do until one night I was talking with Goose and he said to me very poignantly, "Todd, if you think there is something there with Kerri, and I think there is something there, you need to get your butt back to Tuscaloosa and tend to that relationship! Jobs will come and go, but the person you marry is forever." I heard him loud and clear that night and started making plans to move back to Tuscaloosa to figure it out.

When I arrived, I moved right back into my old house with all the same guys who were still students. I laid a mattress on the floor in Lance's room and hit the streets to find a job. I told Kerri I was there to date and pursue her, then I kissed her for the first time to seal the deal. I was determined to handle this relationship in a holy manner and was excited to see what was going to happen.

Now I needed a job, any job. I went back to the country club where I had lifeguarded and they told me I could bartend. Not my first choice, but it would bring tips and I could figure it out from there. But before I could even start that job, I had a friend who said he could get me on as a server at Ruby Tuesday. The hiring manager told me he didn't want to hire me because he knew I would not be there long with my degree, but against his better judgment he said I could train the following week and get started. Alongside this, I had reached out to a local engineering group. After training at Ruby Tuesday for one day, the President of the Engineering Group, Gilbert Sentel, said I could come to work for him, not as a civil engineer, but as a surveyor, actually as a surveyor's helper.

I think the pay was $20,000 a year, but it didn't matter because I was back in Tuscaloosa with all my friends and I was spending all of my free time with the beautiful and fun Miss Kerri Kuiper. By the time November came around, I knew I wanted to marry her.

One evening during that season, though, we did hit an impasse. We were talking about our futures and I began to explain how I was working as an engineer now, but I wanted to be in the ministry in the future, either here in the US or overseas. She replied that was great and admirable, but she would never want to be in the ministry. She had known multiple children of ministers throughout her life and they were all wild and crazy. That was certainly not what she wanted for her kids. Kerri was very family-focused and all she wanted in her life was to be a mom, so the thought of doing anything that might jeopardize that dream and push her kids towards rebellion was unthinkable. It was a tragic night for me. I listened to her say these things and didn't reply at all, but immediately went home and knew I was going to have to break off our relationship. I wanted to marry her, but we were being pulled in two very different directions. The thought of breaking up with her was brutally painful because I loved her deeply, but I knew it had to be done. I determined that I would do it the following day.

The next morning arrived and as I approached my car, I found a note under the wiper blade. Kerri had actually heard her own words as she spoke them to me the night before and had contemplated them all night. When she had said them, I didn't act disappointed or try to rebut them, I just politely heard her out as she talked about her future and her clear disdain for raising PKs, i.e., Pastor's Kids. Often, we have thoughts that roll around in our heads and we hold them to be true, but once we actually speak them, we hear them out loud and immediately realize what we are saying cannot be true even though we have internally assumed it to be true for years. This happened with me and my naive racist beliefs; and it had happened with Kerri that night.

She'd stayed up late to write me this long letter explaining that she knew what she had said, but immediately after saying it she knew how misaligned this was with her newfound faith. She explained how this had always been her stance, but with her new faith this position had to be replaced with a desire to serve God wherever He led and however He wanted, trusting Him to lead her children to faithfulness rather than rebellion. I think I still have the letter, and when I read it that morning I was the happiest man in the world! I was prepared to walk away from our relationship to enter the ministry, but that was going to cut me to the core. God, however, had spoken that night to both of us. He spoke to me by allowing me to see that He truly was number one in my life and if I had to leave this beautiful woman I wanted to marry in order to follow Him, I was ready to do it. He spoke to Kerri by showing her that He was going to transform everything about her life and worldview as a new believer. Once this happened, the deal was done. I went shopping for a ring! I was going to marry this girl. I couldn't stand the thought of losing her and I rejoiced at the thought of having her with me for the rest of my life. These feelings are even truer today than they were in November 1992.

Kerri and I were engaged in January and Sentel Engineering hit financial issues the same month, so I was laid off ten days after our engagement. Fortunately, I had paid cash for the ring! I immediately set about looking for work again and knew I wasn't going to find it in Tuscaloosa. As I was in search-and-hustle mode, I reconnected with Cubb Driggers, the guy who had seen me at my worst as an angry drunk and at my best as a leader in Campus Crusade. His family was prominent in Jacksonville, Florida, so he helped me network in that area. Another roommate, Dave Pagliarulo, had his family do the same in Miami. I went to both areas and did some interviewing and landed a job in Jacksonville with Prosser, Hallock and Kristoff Engineering and Consulting Group. I will never forget how it happened. I had lunch with Pete Hallock and at the end of it he told me he had only worked with one other engineer from the University of Alabama and that guy was stellar, so based on that alone he was going to offer me a position. I was to start in two weeks for $30,000 year.

I took this position on the spot and went back to Tuscaloosa to pack, picking up a hitchhiker along the way so I could share the Gospel with him. His name was Fabrice and he was a Frenchman who had come to America to hitchhike across the county and experience it all. He was on his way to Los Angeles and only spoke broken English, so I convinced him that this was not going to end well for him if he did that, as he would surely be robbed somewhere along the way. So I took him home and he lived with me and my eight roommates for the following two weeks and provided quite a bit of entertainment as he was quite the novelty at the University of Alabama. As I prepared my car to go to Jacksonville, I placed all of my belongings into a small pull-behind U-Haul trailer and hit the road to begin my engineering career, which was just a temporary diversion from the upcoming second missionary journey God was going to deliver to me in the near future. Now, however, I was going to work in Florida and preparing for marriage. I didn't know a single person in Jacksonville and was both excited and nervous about the challenge ahead.

The picture Goose saw of me with Kerri Kuiper and wisely told me to "tend to that relationship"

January 1st, 1994

CHAPTER 11

SECOND MISSIONARY JOURNEY

In Jacksonville, I learned the art of land development and engineering design while working sixty-hour weeks—often from 8 a.m. to midnight. It was now clear why Pete Hallock offered me that job on the spot! They had a pile of work and were extremely understaffed.

Outside of work, I had to adjust to life with adults instead of with college students, which is always a hard transition. I remember being shocked at how sexualized and crude some of the women were in this professional engineering office. I expected that from guys, but it was a little shocking hearing all this locker room talk from both men and women of my parent's age around the table in a professional office setting. It actually reminded me of the construction work sites back in the mill village, though those were male only. As I was settling into this new place and routine, my brother, Hunter, moved down to join me for several months. He and Chief had gotten into a major argument and Hunter got frustrated and decided to move to Florida on a whim. I moved him into my place and he stayed for a few months before returning home. I tried to play peacemaker at that time, but standing between those two at that time was like being a Matador in the ring with two bulls. It was easy to get gored.

During my time in Jacksonville, I met one of my lifelong friends, Sam Pearson, at the First Baptist Church of Jacksonville, Florida. This church and this friendship had a major impact in my life. It was here that I learned so much about the Bible by going to church three times each week to hear either Jerry Vines or Homer Lindsey preach. I loved it because I had never experienced this type of intensive teaching week after week. It was also a time when Sam and I would talk through the faith continually and challenge each other to live it out by serving the inner-city poor in a variety of ways. Some Saturdays we would go buy food and hand it out in the park where the homeless congregated, other times we would go to the homeless shelter or even go out to talk to people door to door.

We had another friend who made a big cross and would drag it around the city and even up and down Jacksonville Beach as a reminder of what Jesus had done. I went with him a few times and it was really interesting because you didn't have to go and engage people, they would come and talk to you. Some of them were angry that you were doing this and they would tell you how judgmental and wrong you were, even though you had not said a word. Others would come and encourage you, as they were inspired by the courage it took. We certainly didn't always get it right, but we were fearless in the things we did.

Personally, a very difficult event for me was the return of my Juvenile Rheumatoid Arthritis (JRA) after a nine year remission. As the doctors had promised, it basically burned out when I was fourteen. I didn't have a single symptom again until nine years later, in 1993. I was jogging on the beach with Kerri when out of nowhere my knees started to hurt. The next day they were swollen, and it was obviously back. I went to a rheumatologist who ran all the tests and confirmed it. I went home and put both fists through the wall in a rage. I'd thought this cursed disease was gone for good, yet now it was back to ruin my life again, at least that's how it felt.

I began taking really strong medicines (Methotrexate, for example) as treatment and pressed forward. Eventually it calmed down a bit and I went to Michigan and married my love on January 1st, 1994. Mother was so frail and sick by this time they barely convinced her to get onto the airplane to Michigan for the wedding, but somehow she made it and we had a great time. Kerri and I left from there and honeymooned in the Pocono Mountains, courtesy of Chief, which was crazy generous of him. Behind the scenes, Kerri and I were now preparing for my second missionary journey, her first, to Russia. The desire to go minister in Russia had never really left for me and I had walked Kerri through the rationale as well. Then we were both challenged to go for it and not overthink it by Chuck and Lisa Snead, Campus Crusade directors at the University of Alabama. We were eating dinner with them one evening and they showed great confidence in us and our ability to make an eternal impact in the lives of college students in Russia. That was very empowering for us so that night, the decision was made and we started the application process.

Campus Crusade was the organization we knew best, so I started there first. Unfortunately, they threw water on my fire right away when they said they would not even entertain our application until we had been married for one year. I couldn't believe they would take such a stance! Didn't they know I was a campus and summer project leader? Surely these rules didn't apply to me! But they did. Just as I was about to hang up in frustration, the lady on the other end of the phone said, "Sorry it is not going to work out with us, but I hear the Navigators will at least look at couples in the first year of marriage and take it on a case-by-case basis." That little opening was all I needed. I called the Navigators right away and secured our spot in their application process. Our plan was to raise support for six months and depart for Russia in July of 1994, but God had His way with us in spite of my impatience because we didn't raise our support in time. That meant we had to wait the full year anyway with a departure date in January of 1995, one year and seven days after our wedding date.

When I told Chief I was now going to forgo my newly launched engineering career in order to raise money and move to Russia as a missionary, he about lost it. He really thought that idea had died when it didn't work out that first summer with Wayne Waddell, but it had not. So he called me multiple nights in a row giving me what I termed at the time "Chief's top ten reasons not to go to Russia." Looking back, he had really good reasons. What if Kerri gets pregnant? What if Russia becomes hostile to us again? What if your arthritis flares and you can't get medical attention? He became so upset about it, he asked his friend, a retired FBI agent, to investigate the Navigators. He also secretly called one of the pastors at the church where we were attending, Pastor Doug

Pigg, to find out if they were manipulating me in some way (Doug only told me about these phone conversations several years later). Chief was certainly glad I was no longer in danger of being killed or going to jail via addiction, but he also wanted me to be rational about my newfound faith and not let it "ruin my life and career." He wanted a me to have a measured faith, but I have always been an all or nothing idealist.

Pastor Doug did a great job of talking him off the cliff and reminding him that I was young, but I was also smart and responsible, with enough maturity to make the right decision for my family. After multiple talks with me and his clandestine conversation with Doug, Chief called his FBI agent friend and told him, "Whatever you have found out, don't tell me because Todd is going to do it regardless. I'd rather not know." He knew I was just as headstrong as him. This is comical now because the Navigators are well-known for their integrity in ministry and finances, but for folks from the mill village of Alabama City, the thought of raising well over a year's salary ($48,000) and giving it to an organization in Colorado to send you to Russia for a year certainly sounds like a scam. I don't fault Chief for poking around and asking questions trying to protect me, and I understand his fear and anxiety, watching me seemingly throw away the education he had worked so hard to provide and the degree he valued so much, especially since he never finished his college education. Chief only shared these things with me over a decade later when I was in my thirties. By that time, he had made peace with my calling and at times he was even proud of what I was doing with my life.

Pastor Doug was a mentor to me during this season of life. He was a great man who taught me so much week after week in our newlywed Sunday School class, and I really admired him. I told him my plan to go to Russia with the Navigators and then to attend Dallas Theological Seminary to train for ministry. He heard me out and then started really challenging everything I had just told him. He asked why I was going to Russia and if I thought I would be effective there. He asked how and why I had chosen Dallas Theological Seminary? He went further and said, "By all means, the church needs men to serve in all kinds of roles, but what the church doesn't need is to have men and women there who are not called of God!" He then asked me if I'd had any specific time in my life when I was clearly "called of God."

I wasn't familiar with that "calling" lingo and couldn't relay any type of experience to that effect. I think I even told him I wasn't called by God, but rather I was volunteering for God. That didn't fit his theological matrix at all, so he told me I was a great young man, but if I didn't have a specific calling experience then I wasn't called at all and should probably do something else. I remember him using the old refrain, "If there is anything else in the world you can do other than ministry and be happy, do that! This is not an easy path and if you are not called, you will not last. But if you are called, this is the absolute only thing you can do in life and you should know it."

His words came down on me like a sledgehammer, almost shattering the vision I had for my life and ministry. At that time in my life, I knew I could do other things, I just didn't want to do them. I wanted to do ministry, but I didn't have any direct calling experience. I'd had Chuck and Lisa Snead, folks who had seen me grow from a hellion into a Christian influencer, tell me that a year in Russia sharing Jesus with other college students would be a great investment of my life. They thought I would be really effective there. That was not exactly a Divine experience, though, with thunderclaps or voices of angels.

Doug also really pressed me to consider Southeastern Baptist Theological Seminary over Dallas Theological Seminary, saying Southeastern was on the rise and would be about 50 percent of the cost of Dallas Theological. I had never heard of Southeastern Baptist and told him I would consider it, but preeminent in my mind as I left his office that day was, *Am I really called to ministry? Have I been mistaken about what is involved with this? Should I consider just going to Russia for a year and then coming home to be an engineer in light of the fact that I have no specific calling experience?*

As I drove back to my engineering office, I was confused as I tearfully and angrily reached out to God. "If you really want me to do this, I am up for it, but I don't have to do it! And if Doug is so set on my having some type of experiential calling, then maybe that's what is necessary, and I just won't go to seminary without that. If You want me to do it, You show me! Otherwise, I will just tap out and not go. I don't want to make a huge mistake." I remember it well. It was hard. I was feeling as though I had to give up on this vision I'd had for my life since college and it felt like a death.

I can't provide specific timetables, but within the next thirty days two significant events happened to revive the vision and give me confidence moving forward. First, I was talking to Mother about something related to church one evening on the telephone. I don't remember exactly what it was, but something in the spiritual realm. This was that time in her life when she was still lucid, but emotionally and cognitively fragile. In the midst of this conversation, she just blurted out, "Todd, you are going to be a preacher, aren't you? I just knew you were going to be a preacher. I am so proud of you." Again, I don't remember what we were discussing, but we were not discussing my becoming a preacher. But it just came out and she was crying when she said it.

The second event happened within days of the first. It was midweek, so I took a few hours away from work and went to hear some preaching at an annual conference that First Baptist Jacksonville hosted. As I was in the parking lot on my way into the church, an older gentleman walked right up to me out of the blue and said, "Hey, young man, where did you get those seminary shoes? You must be a seminary student with those shoes?"

I answered, "No, I'm just a member of the church here."

The man kept walking with no further conversation. I was a little stunned. The shoes I had on were normal black wing tips. As a matter of fact, I had bought them at a secondhand store in Gadsden several years ago because I didn't have money to buy new ones at that time. Maybe he saw how old they looked and thought I must be in seminary? The more plausible answer, given that almost everyone wore black wing tips at that time, was that God had orchestrated these events to subtly affirm my direction and remove the doubts. He had put me through a gut-wrenching exercise of counting the cost of ministry through Doug's challenge, and after weeks of ambiguity about who I was and what I was supposed to do, God had burst the bubble of tension. He was releasing me to do what that mystery man and my mother had told me to do without any solicitation, namely, go to Russia and then enter seminary.

These were my first lessons in what it meant to exercise faith and it led to our entire faith journey. Kerri and I would move forward from this place and exercise faith throughout the next year by raising support to go to Russia. We also learned to serve together. I didn't really know what else to do, so we went to several nursing homes and asked if they had residents who never received guests. Of course they did so we started to visit two of these ladies in the evenings several times a month. One of them was named Zettie and she was a lot of fun. Looking back, I am sure these wide eyed twenty somethings brought some joy into her life as we visited and made conversation then ended in prayer. Everything great starts small, so if you want to do great things find some small things you can do in a great way. During this season of life, that is what we did, from visiting in nursing homes to taking children from our apartment complex to the fair to feeding the homeless in the parks. If small acts of service are too small for you, then great leadership is beyond your reach.

During this first year of marriage, I saw clearly mother's mental and emotional decline both over the phone and in person on the occasional visit home. As a "fixer", I found an in-patient treatment center for depression and other mental illnesses and thought this could solve the problem. Somehow, I managed to fly Mother down to Florida and took her to this Christian treatment center, called Rapha, which was an hour or so outside of Jacksonville. She was so frail and nervous about what was going to happen, but she trusted me enough to try it. Once we arrived, she really didn't want to stay at the center and I had to constantly reassure her that it was going to be okay. I confidently told her that these people were going to help her, even though internally I started to get anxious myself. After all, I didn't know any of these people, but I knew everyone there was really sick. Mother was desperately paranoid about being somewhere and them tying her down and giving her electric shock treatments. I had to constantly reassure her that this was not going to happen to her here, just as a parent reassures an irrational toddler about being in the dark. But as a twenty-five-year-old, I was in way over my head.

Looking back, I don't even remember how many days Mother remained there. I do remember riding away after leaving her there and driving through a McDonald's where I opened the car door to throw up because my stomach was in such a knot from violently crying. I felt so alone in that moment because I was feeling her aloneness. I felt so scared because I knew she was scared. At this time, I was still very angry at Chief because I naively viewed him as the single cause of Mother's pain, and I was emotionally destroyed by all of this tragedy.

I was initially hopeful her stint at Rapha would be the magic bullet to pull her out of her depression, but upon leaving her there I began to lose all hope. I made a few calls to her early in her stay, and she told me about some types of group therapy and the like, and that they were trying to regulate the many prescription medicines she was taking. I think I had her scheduled to be there for several weeks, but I don't think she made it the entire time. At some point, I went and took her from the inpatient treatment center and brought her to our apartment, where Kerri graciously cared for her. She just loved Kerri and knew that I had married way over my head. She may have stayed one night before I was forced to put her back on a plane to fly home to Gadsden. Her physical and mental capacity were slipping rapidly, as was my hope for any recovery or joy in her life going forward. I so desperately wanted her to regain some portion of joy in life and wanted to solve that problem so badly, but this option had failed. I would not give up so easily, however, and would keep trying against all odds, though when no one was watching, I cried . . . a lot.

⁊ • ⁊

After completing support raising in December, we were able to travel home to Gadsden, Alabama to see my family before eventually departing for Russia from Michigan, where Kerri's family lives. We made it to Russia the first week of January 1995. It was my first trip out of the country and it was for a one-year term. Previously, we'd met our teammates in Charlotte, North Carolina, for a week of training before being sent to Blagoveshchensk, a city in the far east of Russia on the Chinese border. Blagoveshchensk, interestingly enough, means "city of good news." Everyone on our team was anxious and ready to share the good news throughout this city, as I think we all expected it to be really easy because we had heard that everyone in the former Soviet Union was eager and ready to receive Jesus and follow Him after seventy years of Communism. Unfortunately, that was fake news, but we didn't know it at the time. It was actually better that we didn't know it, as that would have curbed our enthusiasm. Billy Swanson, along with his wife, Lolly, and his children, was our team leader. He was the most optimistic, energetic guy I had ever known. He made it a lot of fun for everyone at all times. Stephen Coney was a really high-IQ guy with whom I enjoyed discussing theology and philosophy and he taught me a lot. There were others as well, all of whom had a great impact on my life. All in all, we had a team of ten adults and six kids, and it was an incredibly transformational year in our lives.

Living in a new culture with few relational contacts provided me with a lot of time in which to read more than ever, and to learn unique cultural customs. One of these is called the "Banya." We were taken to a personal Banya at a camp by one of our translators, Tatiana. She was a woman in her sixties and she had with her a brother and sister-in-law along with me and Kerri. In a Russian Banya, the goal is to sweat out your impurities and strengthen your heart. You first go into a steaming hot sauna unlike you have ever experienced. It is so hot, in fact, that we wore a cloth toboggan to cover our ears to keep them from burning. You sit there for a few minutes until you are about to pass out, at which point Tatiana's brother breaks out a small branch from a tree with lots of leaves still on it. He takes this branch and begins to beat you with it, the strikes not hurting at all, but the hot air generated by each swing feeling like boiling death. This goes on for a minute or so, at which point you are invited to return the favor and beat him with the branch. Then, just seconds before passing out, you run out of the sauna and jump into an icy-cold pool, or go roll around in the snow if you can't afford a pool. This coolness feels really good for about ten milliseconds, and then it is so cold it hurts, so you pull yourself out of the pool and run back toward the sauna to take another scalding hot beating. You do this about three times in a row, at which point you go upstairs and drink hot tea with cookies. Then you repeat the entire exercise at least two or three more times, at which point you literally cannot move because your entire body is Jell-O. Tatiana then reminds you of how good this is for your health, although the doctor on our team reminded us of the stress it put on the heart. Either way, it was very memorable, especially since Tatiana, her brother and sister-in-law totally stripped down to their birthday suits for the exercise while Kerri and I opted to stay in swimsuits, for which we were continuously chastised by our hosts. A very memorable experience for sure.

Outside of these great cultural experiences, I found myself with significant time to write more than a book in journaling. It was before the internet existed for the general public, so our only connection back home was letters, with those only coming in and out every six weeks. This lack of communication with anyone in America isolated me and Kerri so that we really bonded together. We walked everywhere we went, survived crazy drivers when we did hail a cab, and learned to live as foreigners in a strange land. There were times when I had nothing to do so I would walk around this town and go to the statues of Vladimir Lenin and pray against the forces of evil that had robbed this country of Gospel influence for decades through Communism.

The greatest thing to come out of this time in Russia was Lena. Not our daughter Laina, but her namesake, Lena Petrovna. Lena was a French and English student at the local university where we were doing ministry and she came to our Bible studies faithfully. At some point in that process, she clearly heard and understood the Gospel, just as I had with Bard back at the University of Alabama. Immediately, she began to grow in her faith. She subsequently led her friend, Sveta, to faith as well. I always thought of her like Lydia, whom Paul met on one of his missionary journeys, as she became for us a real bridge to the culture. In addition to seeing several students embrace the faith, our team was also able to start a small new congregation in the city. For a bunch of novices thrown together for a hurried one-week training with no Russian language skills at all, it was a great success. Twenty years later many of those same people continue to walk with God and proclaim His message.

Lena's complete faith story is certainly worth recounting at this point, and it is best to hear it in her own words. I asked her to write it out for me in some correspondence we had in 2001 so that I could share it with our daughter as she got older. I remember her describing how she had no access to a Bible anywhere in her village, but at some point she gained access to parts of the Old Testament and read it, though it did not make sense to her. Following that, her heart was very much inclined toward God, but she had no idea how to really know Him, pray to Him, or make peace with Him. She even got on a train with Sveta and traveled far away to a Russian Orthodox Church to try and find God. Upon arriving at the church, she bought some candles to burn incense and was baptized as well as given a small cross. What she was not given was any real explanation of the Gospel. She was indeed like the Ethiopian eunuch spoken about in the book of Act in the New Testament who wanted to know and understand the words of God but had no teacher. Phillip had been sent to the Ethiopian Eunuch and we had been sent to Lena. Read her words below exactly as she wrote them.

Kerri and your big family, hello.

How are you doing? What's new? I work at the International Service of Congratulations. The studying is over and all our young people are at the Christian camp now. We are preparing to the youth camp at August. Would you like to come? My dream is to see you some day with your kids, especially Laina. I want to give my testimony so she could know about me.

I was born (1973, September 26) in a family of good people, simple and kind. I've got my older sister Tanya, she's thirty-four now. I used to be a pioneer, then a Komsomol member. We were taught that there is now [sic] God, but very deep in my hea[r]t I believed that He was. If I said at school about my faith, they would laughed at me. So I finished the school, went to the city of Blagoveshchensk to study French and English at the Institute. In 1994 I knew that my father began drinking alcohol. He was very close to me, an example, I wanted to be like he, he taught me many things, more than my mother. Can you imagine what was with me? Then my mother. They needed money and they sold almost everything in our house. They didn't help me (financially) to live in another city as all parents did. They were my hope, my support and I felt abandoned, without them I couldn't do anything. I was ashamed to tell about it to my friends, even to my close friend Sveta. Finally, I told her and she helped me. But there was an emptiness inside of me, a big grief. At that moment I met two missionaries from US who told me about God and His love, I began reading the Bible. I didn't doubt that it was the truth. I decided to trust the Lord, because without Him all is [in] vain. I can't control my life by myself, nobody can. Everything that we trust on can be destroyed, is not eternal. Even my family which was very good, respected, known in our small town. I didn't really think about my sins, I just wanted to have God as my Lord, Support, Hope and tried to please Him by living how He wants me to live. You know what was then—Sveta came and repented. It was one of the first great examples of God's care. Together we became stronger, ran from the sin. Maybe you understood that we had some friends who were taking us away from God, but your prayers and others were stronger. I understood that I couldn't live partly and I turned away from all that was bad. At school I was a leader, I was responsible for many things. That's why I couldn't just go to the church, seat on the bench. I wanted devote all my life to the Lord and I went to the Far East Bible college where I received more than I expected, I met Kostya! [Her future husband]

Our desire now is to help other people come to Christ as you did for me, Sveta: thank God for His wise plan.

What about you health, Kerri? Lena.

During this year in Russia, I only spoke with my family two or three times, though I did write some letters. Long distance calls from Russia cost six dollars per minute at that time! This left me out of the loop on much that was going on at home, but this was a great season of growth for me personally. Near the end of our term, I received a message that Mama White had passed away. It was really difficult to miss this funeral and my family at that time. After this, Papa Ed trailed off into worse and worse dementia so it was as if he had died as well. Those two were my childhood refuge from all the chaos in our own house and now they were gone. By all accounts Mother was no better nor worse, though the loss of Mama White was devastating for her.

Toward the end of this first year in Russia, Kerri and I had two very important decisions to make. First, we had to decide on our career path going forward. Our options were to pursue a full-time role as international missionaries or to attend seminary and pursue a more traditional ministry role in the US. Secondly, we had to consider whether it was time to have children. The first decision was difficult for us because we were young in our marriage and we hyper-spiritualized most things at this time. Thus, we decided to pray and ask the Lord individually for a month about our future career and at the end of that time we would come together to see if we were on the same page. I would never give that advice to a young couple today, as I would want them to wrestle through it together as one, but that was the plan we came up with and we followed through with it.

By the time we arrived at month's end, we were truly experiencing the highs and lows of missionary life. On the high side, Lena and Sveta and others had truly embraced the faith and we were doing all kinds of outreach projects together with them. We had cookouts in our courtyards and even started a small church that met on Sunday nights. On the low side, we were really missing our families, as we had only spoken to them a few times during the entire past year. We were also ready to be done with the minus-thirty-degree days for which we were ill-equipped. Even so, we had both come to the same conclusion—missionary work was our calling and we were going to pursue it wholeheartedly.

The second decision was whether or not we were going to stop using birth control and begin our family. I will never forget our supervisor, Brad Hillman, coming over to our house to check on us, as he did every six weeks when he came to visit. Brad was a great man, very wise and a lot of fun. He would fly over to Russia and travel around the far east region to check up on the thirty Navigator missionaries serving in that area. I remember clearly telling him that we were thinking of starting a family and wondering if it was a good time, as we still had about four months left in the country before finishing our term. I was asking because we had agreed to put off trying to get pregnant as a part of our application process for this one-year term. I concluded by asking, "So do you think we should try once or twice before we leave here and return home?" obviously meaning one or two monthly cycles. Brad just grinned real big and with a twinkle in his eye replied, "Oh, I would definitely try more than once or twice!" With his blessing, we stopped all birth control and began to pursue pregnancy. Like most couples, we assumed it would happen in one month, two at the most. And like many couples, we were dead wrong. I still remember taking a pregnancy test every month for the last several months we were in Russia and having negative tests and all of the negative emotions and anxieties that follow that experience. So we started around October 1995, and finally got pregnant ten months later, in August 1996.

Making these two very impactful decisions during the last few months of the second missionary journey set us up for the next season of life at Southeastern Baptist Theological Seminary in Wake Forest, North Carolina. We had visited there at Doug Pigg's request right before going overseas and we were thrilled to jump into this new experience together. I was in my theological "season of the mind" with a thousand questions for which I just knew I could find an answer if I only thought, studied and read enough. With these unrealistic expectations, I was totally set up for seminary life.

Over the next two years I would read hundreds of books and dialogue thousands of hours with professors and other students around matters theological, philosophical, political, and sociological. It was a very formative experience for both of us, which launched us into our third and final missionary journey. We initially thought this third missionary journey would be to Pakistan or India, but at the last minute it was redirected by our seminary back to Central Asia. Most of the Central Asian sites were in the various 'Stans of that region (e.g. Kazakhstan, Tajikistan, etc.), but one was located in Russia proper, so it was an easy choice for us to return to Russia. At this point, we assumed we would spend the rest of our lives there as career missionaries. Our other assumption was that the Russia we were returning to in 1998 would be the same Russia we had left at the end of 1995. Neither assumption turned out to be true, as is often the case when you make life plans in your twenties.

First few days in Russia without a washer & dryer

Blagoveshchensk, Russia

CHAPTER 12

FINAL SECRETS UNVEILED

When we returned to the States in December 1995, we moved immediately to Wake Forest, North Carolina to start seminary. We drove into town with a little money and a few pieces of furniture, but nowhere to live. There was very little available that we could afford, so we landed in a mobile home park out in the country, in Youngsville. It was a single-wide with two bedrooms and not a sliver of insulation anywhere! Kerri found a job as a teaching assistant right away and I went to work as a customer service representative in a UPS call center to make ends meet. With $400 in electric bills on top of a $400 rent payment, it took a lot to make those ends meet! Meanwhile, back at home, Mother's mental illness and decline were steadily progressing and the darkest days were still ahead of us.

During my first semester, I remember calling Mother often.

Most of the time she would be crying and fearful. She was scared about her health, she was lonely, she was unbelievably sad, and she was in steep decline. Toward the end of the semester, I decided that Kerri and I needed to go back home to spend the summer living in our house on 3704 Roselawn Drive with Mother and Daddy. Looking back, I can't believe Kerri said yes so easily to this incredible request, but she has always supported me in a unique and unconditional manner.

I had come to this conclusion on another night I will never forget. I was in our trailer alone and Daddy called to say that he had to have Mother committed to the local psychiatric facility, Mountain View Hospital. I could often calm Mother down when she was really fearful, so he arranged for me to call to her there. We spoke briefly and as usual, she was crying. She was very scared, and I had no idea what they were doing with her. When I think of Mountain View Hospital, I think of two guys from there who came to talk to us in high school about killing their parents, so I didn't associate anything positive with the place.

After talking to me just a few minutes, Mother put the phone down abruptly, almost hanging up on me. I could tell she was very confused with what was happening there. I heard her voice trail off talking to someone else, as she couldn't even hang up the telephone receiver. The sound of her voice trailing off, talking to some orderly, and her being so confused and fearful, hit me in a way that nothing had since I buried Jason Brown in high school. I remember lying on the floor of that mobile home in the middle of nowhere and crying harder and longer than I ever had. Because she was alone and afraid, I felt alone and afraid. I also knew that all her other relationships were gone after years of depression and isolation. I began to reason that if she was going to have any joy going forward, Kerri and I would have to bring it to her. Therefore, the decision was made. We moved home that summer and lived in my brother's old bedroom.

Mother was so excited that we were coming home! I had been trying to care for her from a distance since leaving home in 1989 and now it was time to come home and give focused help for a season. I worked for Daddy that summer back in residential remodeling once again, but that was not why I was there. I was there for my mother, and my wife was there for me. It was a very hard summer, sharing a very small home with my parents, but it was the right thing to do and I am so glad that we did it.

When I think back on that summer, I recall how uncomfortable I often made my brother and Chief at the time. They were uncomfortable with me because they didn't really know how to treat me. When I was in high school and college, I was the craziest of the three of us, drinking to excess, smoking pot, fighting, etc. But now I was the family preacher who was going to seminary and had been overseas as a missionary. The one who used to have the filthy mouth now walked away from the dirty jokes. The one who liked to party now liked to go to church. It was weird for all of us because I had not really been home for such a long stretch in many years. My brother coped with it primarily by making fun of me. I'll never forget, he called me Forest Gump all summer because now I was so straight. It used to make me fighting mad because he knew I was neither naive nor "holier than thou," but he pretended as though I had totally forgotten the first twenty-one years of my life and now I was this untouchable holy man. I had done the same to Goose years earlier, but it was incredibly aggravating to be on the other side. Folks I worked with on the construction sites piled on as well, so it was lonely and frustrating at work. It didn't matter, though, because I was there primarily for Mother, not them. I had to do something to help her and this was all I knew to do for her, to come home and spend time with her and try to bring her some joy.

One day I was sitting in our construction office and my Uncle Bill walked in, as he was visiting from Florida. He probably hadn't seen me in four or five years and had heard about my conversion experience and newfound religion. When he came in, he greeted me and immediately said, "I heard you got religion," or something similar. I said that I had found Jesus and decided to worship Him, as I hated the baggage that went along with the word *religion*. Then he said, "Good for you, but you keep that shit away from me, I don't want any part of it." Seriously? I didn't bring it up with him, he brought it up with me. I had just said hello, but he pounced right away because no one knew what to do with me now that I was this holy man. This was sadly the last time I ever spoke to my Uncle Bill and he died several years later after a heart transplant.

Daddy loved Uncle Bill like a brother, as they lived so much of their lives connected and they were very similar. I'll never forget when Daddy told me how he called down to Uncle Bill when Bill was in his very last days of life in Florida. According to Daddy, he called specifically to talk to him about his eternity. I was shocked for two reasons. First, what was Daddy doing talking to someone about their soul? He'd basically mocked me for doing that. Two, how could he do that with Uncle Bill, who basically told me to shove it before I even started the conversation. Daddy said he called Bill and said, "Bill, I know that you know you are dying and I am worried about you. I know you don't believe in the whole Jesus thing, but WHAT IF IT IS ACTUALLY TRUE? That is a hell of a chance to take if it happens to be true, Bill. Why not pray and make peace with God just in case?" When Daddy said this my mouth hit the floor. This is not the way I would talk to someone who was dying, but I was shocked that Daddy was so concerned for Uncle Bill's soul that he at least thought there was a chance this stuff was true. I don't know if Bill chose to hear these words from his lifelong friend or not. I sure hope he did. Within just a few days, Uncle Bill was gone.

At the end of this summer at home, just a few days before leaving, I sat out on our porch one last time with Mother. Our little concrete porch had green indoor/outdoor carpet on it and we often sat there in the afternoon. The porch is way too small for chairs, so we always sat on the steps. By this time, Mother was sometimes more coherent than other times, and on this day she was totally aware and coherent. She told me some things I had never heard before, things that tortured my soul. She told me that she was raped right after high school. I don't know all the particulars, but she and a friend went out to some club in or around Madison or Huntsville, Alabama. Two guys followed her home that night and broke into her house and raped her. *How in the hell did this happen and how did none of us ever know about it?* I thought. She said that they actually had a criminal trial, or maybe the guys took a plea bargain, but as best I could tell they got off with a slap on the wrist, as was often the case in the 1950's, and even today, much to our shame as a society.

Looking back now, this tragedy in Mother's life explains so much. It explains her low self-esteem, her chasing the bad guy, Chief, because often when a woman has been raped they believe the despicable lie that good guys will no longer want them. It explains that night at Pasquales Restaurant when I was eleven-years-old and we'd stopped to eat there. That night we had just finished playing a soccer game nearby and as usual, it was just me, Mother, and Hunter. As we were getting into our car to leave, Mother said to Hunter, "Hurry up, son, your Daddy is going to be here in just a minute."

Hunter was confused and replied something along the lines of, "What are you talking about?"

Mother then said, "Your Daddy is coming right away!"

We all piled into our old Ford Thunderbird car and Mother immediately locked the doors. I could see she was visibly shaken and as we drove off hastily, Mother said to us both very sternly, "If I ever say your dad is coming or we are going to meet your dad, you always reply 'yes' and move quickly to get into the car. There were two men in there watching me closely and they walked out right behind us. They could be dangerous, so don't ever argue with me when I say something like that." At the time, none of that made any sense to me, as I never even saw the two men. But now, almost 15 years later, after hearing her story of being raped, I understood.

I didn't know how to process all that she was telling me that day, so I just listened. She was crying and I was as well. Fifteen years after Mother's death, I would ask Daddy about Mother being raped and what he knew about it. He said it was true, but he knew very little about it other than tidbits her parents had shared with him. I asked if he ever discussed it with her and he replied, "Never." They were married almost forty years and it was never discussed! I asked him why they had never discussed it and he said, "It was her story and she never brought it up, so I never felt free to ask." Rape was such a stigma at that time so the victims were forced to suffer in silence. It was and is such an evil system. I called a few of my mom's living friends a while back to ask if they knew anything about her rape and they all said they didn't know anything about it. That meant she literally suffered in silence for more than forty years. Rape is such a horrible crime. God is just, and there is nothing hidden that will not be revealed, and He will repay.

Mother kept talking as we sat there together and I asked her about Chief's religious experiences. I had often heard at one point in his life he stopped drinking for a season, proclaimed his faith, and was even baptized.

He began to talk to his friends about Jesus and forgiveness. She said it was true, that at some point early in their marriage, well before I was born, Chief somehow embraced the Christian faith. I think this happened through some of his friends, and he seemingly went all in. He stopped drinking, cussing, and sleeping around cold turkey. He began to tell his drinking buddies how good it was to follow Jesus and was baptized in a small church in East Gadsden, Louis Street Baptist Church. The pastor was a man named Rev. Welch (we always called him Brother Welch) and Daddy really liked him because he was also a quail hunter. As Mother continued talking, she was smiling and remembering how great those months or perhaps even a year was for them. They had friends in a Sunday School class and they used to get together and play cards on the weekends and have good clean fun for the first time since they were in high school. Daddy was so naturally charismatic they had him teaching the students at church and praying opening prayers at the beginning of Sunday services very soon after his baptism, which was a terrible mistake. I have no idea how long this went on, but my assumption is that it lasted close to a year. Then it happened—the event that would change the trajectory of our family forevermore. Initially it doesn't seem that sinister, but its results were devastating: Daddy got drunk.

Mother was continuing to cry as she explained the scenario to me. She said Daddy had been sober for so long and was doing so well, but then he slipped off and got drunk one night. Not a binge drunk, just a single day. When he sobered up, the guilt he felt was immense. Here he was, a teacher of the youth at church, a leader of prayer on Sundays, and the one who had been calling on his friends to stop drinking and come to church with him. This is the exact reason the Bible says you are not to put a young, new believer in a public position of authority. They are young and can easily slip back into an old sin. If they slip while they are still out of the spotlight there is certainly guilt, but not paralyzing guilt. Alternatively, when they are already in the spotlight and proclaiming their faith publicly and teaching others as a leader, the guilt of this type of mistake can be paralyzing. That was the case with Chief.

Brother Welch did all the right things at this time according to Mother. He came to Daddy and told him that it was just a slip, it wasn't a fall, and he was forgiven. He told him to not let this single event curse him, but to get up again and keep following the path of Jesus that he had chosen. Unfortunately, the damage was done. Daddy seemingly lost hope. When that happens, all hell breaks loose, as it is written in the Scriptures, "Just as a freshly washed sow returns to the mud" and "as a dog returns to his vomit, so a fool returns to his folly" (*New International Version*, 1 Pet 2.22). And so it was with H. M. Carnes, a man with so much promise as a Christian leader. He went right back into his crazy lifestyle of shame, anger, and addiction, becoming twice the hellion that he was previous to this. That is why things were so violent and horrific in our house in the years that followed.

A man is very dangerous to himself and others when he loses hope in both God and himself, which is no doubt what happened to Daddy at this tragic point in his life. It didn't have to be that way, as he could have received forgiveness and kept marching forward in his faith, but he didn't. Episodes like this should act as a reminder to us all that our churches must be grace filled and absolutely full of forgiveness, not judgment.

After Mother relayed these heavy things to me that day sitting on our porch, I remember mourning in isolation for weeks, for I couldn't reveal these family secrets to anyone. As a matter of fact, I don't think I spoke of them for many years, not even to my wife. Family secrets were just that, secrets. Meanwhile, I was mourning what could have been for our family. What would have happened if Daddy would have received God's unconditional forgiveness and stepped right back into the church that next Sunday and became an even bigger proponent of grace for folks like himself? What would have happened if my brother and I had grown up going to Louis Street Baptist church instead of being tortured in a home of addiction and violence? What would it have been like to see Mother and Daddy happy and hanging out with sober friends rather than having a house constantly filled with chaos, violence and drunkenness? What would Mother's health and emotional recovery have been like if she had enjoyed a nurturing marriage for the last thirty years instead of an abusive one? What could have been? It hurt deeply then; it still hurts today.

I am glad Mother peeled back the outer layer of her life and bared her soul to me that day, as it explained so much that I never understood. I never told anyone about the rape story until I asked Chief about it one day some fifteen years later. It was too intimate, too personal, and again, for me to even say it caused this wave of shame and anger to come over me that I could not handle emotionally. As Mother's protector, I didn't feel like I could say anything about it unless I was committed to hunting down the guys who did it and beating them senseless, and I had no way to find them without dragging Mother back through it all. I can't fully explain the anger it brings and I hope you never experience it.

I remember getting up to leave our conversation and realizing this was going to be the last lucid conversation I would ever have with my mother. I was going back to seminary the next day and wouldn't be back at home for four months. I didn't expect her to be lucid when I returned, and that was indeed the case. She delivered these last few insights into her life and her pain right there on our porch at 3704 Roselawn Drive, the most appropriate place. This conversation is always with me and it serves as a constant reminder of all that is at stake when I am talking to young couples about the Gospel and the impact it can have not only on them, but on generations to come. This is why I do premarital counseling free of charge for any couple that will sign up because I want to be a protector of those future generations. I know all too well what is at stake for the children who will be born into that home.

Within a year mother had to be placed in a full-time nursing facility at the very young age of fifty-eight. Her dementia was progressing rapidly, her sadness was too much to bear, and she was beginning to have real episodes of paranoia. Just before she went to the nursing facility, I came home one weekend to find that she had run away from Mama Zana's house because she thought they were trying to kill her. I went to pick her up from the local community center, where she was "hiding." At first, she came to me and trusted me, but soon she was even having doubts about me, whether or not I was going to help them harm her. Once again, I died a little that night. I wanted so badly for her to be happy and able to rest, but it was over. The rest of her life was going to be a living hell of loneliness, paranoia, and ultimately total disassociation from reality. She went into the nursing facility just as I was finishing up seminary and Kerri and I were preparing to move back to Russia with the International Mission Board for a two-year term. I felt as if I would never see Mother again nor be at her funeral when we left home that last time on our way back to Russia in November 1998. I took an old picture frame and printed out the verses from the Gospel of John 14:1–3 on a plain piece of paper and placed it on the wall of her tiny 10' x 10' room.

> *Do not let your hearts be troubled. You believe in God; believe also in me. My Father's house has many rooms; if that were not so, would I have told you that I am going there to prepare a place for you? And if I go and prepare a place for you, I will come back and take you to be with me that where I am, you may be also.*

As I left her small room, I was driving away alone when I saw her through the exterior window of her room. I weep even now as I write this, and I am sure I will weep every single time I read it. The image of her in that tiny room all alone haunts me. It was a thousand times more painful than all the whippings I endured. The pain of that moment was not the pain of not seeing her again, as I didn't want her to live long in that desperate place. Rather, it was the pain of feeling all of her loneliness and fear and insecurity in my soul and not begin able to do a single thing about it. It was devastating then, it still is today.

Against all odds, Mother survived in the nursing home the entire two years we were in Russia. When we returned, we brought our daughter, Laina, to see her. By now she no longer knew who we were, but oh, how she loved little Laina. When people have dementia, they develop this faraway look in their eyes. They don't really look at you anymore, they just look off into space even as they try to talk with you. This is how I remember interacting with Mother at this time. Her lucid days were gone forever and she was soon going to be confined to her bed, wearing diapers. This is exactly what happened for twelve additional months, before she would finally, mercifully pass from this life into the next.

Mother's last few days at home, holding her granddaughter, Laina

The porch of our home at 3704 Roselawn Drive where we sat and talked

CHAPTER 13

ANGELS IN SCRUBS

In my final year of seminary, I was completing my coursework and we had saved just enough money so that neither of us were working during these final few months in the US. That allowed Kerri to stay home with our newborn daughter, Laina, while we prepared for our upcoming missionary career. At this time we were thrilled to find out Kerri was now pregnant with our second child. Soon we discovered it was going to be a boy and I chose the perfect name for him, Jason Todd Carnes, in honor of my best high school friend who had died. As the summer was approaching and we were preparing to go to the Russian Language Institute at Columbia International University, Kerri suddenly started to have complications. We were in Gadsden visiting my family when the complications became very serious. Kerri wound up in the office of Dr. Grimes, OB-GYN, who happened to be the father of one of my elementary school classmates. Dr. Grimes evaluated Kerri and said the pregnancy was tenuous at best and admitted her to the hospital immediately. She was there for several days and they told us that her amniotic sack had ruptured, though most of the fluid had not leaked out and the baby was still healthy. As she was discharged, Dr. Grimes said she would need bedrest for the rest of the pregnancy. Bedrest with no home and no bed, plus an energetic one-year-old, is a hard thing to accomplish. But as Chief always said, "There are two things you can always do, son. Things you really want to do, and things you have to do!" We had to figure it out.

We left Gadsden and made it to Columbia, South Carolina in June 1998. Upon arrival we went to the duplex I had rented for the summer, sight unseen. Previous Russian Language students had rented it, a couple of guys, so I assumed it was going to be fine. It was not. When we arrived, we realized that we were in a very tough section of town. We probably only had a suitcase between us plus all of Laina's necessities. We unloaded and went into the duplex and quickly realized it was going to be a long summer. The duplex was very small, had almost no yard, and only had window AC units to labor through the very hot Columbia summer. We were determined to make it work, though, primarily because we didn't have other options.

I went to classes for about a week and worried about Kerri and Laina the entire time. After only one week, we found ourselves out on the small porch giving Laina some time to run around in the front yard when we saw a drug deal going down catty-corner to us on our street. That was it, the straw that broke the camel's back. I called the landlord and explained to him that I had no idea this was what was happening in and around this duplex and there was no way I was going to leave my pregnant wife and child here during the daytime hours alone. He knew exactly what I was talking about and didn't even put up an argument. I told him he could keep whatever money I had sent as a deposit if he needed to, but we had to go. He returned the deposit and we wound up moving into the student housing dorms for International Students at Ben Lippen School for the summer, escaping the drug deals and the hot nights.

With our new living arrangement in place, things were much better. We were living somewhat communally with other single students, but at least we had our own room and bathroom and felt safe. We adjusted to this communal scenario and Laina had a great time feeding the ducks at the pond next to the housing. It was during this time I began to realize just how strong and industrious my wife is. Kerri is a natural optimist and always finds a way in difficult circumstances. Here, she would take Laina outdoors to play with the garden hose, she would take her to the closest McDonald's to play in the play place (where she often got stuck in the ball pit because she was only twelve months old), and they'd find other activities. This particular season of life, along with her husband's singularly focused ambition, had given her lemons and she'd made lemonade. This was the state of affairs when Kerri went for her OB/GYN appointment at about six and a half months due to some new spotting. Her pregnancy had somewhat returned to normal after several months in Columbia so she was back up and around and seemingly doing well. This day, however, was different. I can still see her physician's face, as he was an Alabama graduate with whom I had talked football, of course. This day he had really bad news.

They had gone looking for little Jason's heartbeat and couldn't find it. He had died in the womb at seven months. So we found ourselves in Columbia, South Carolina, a place we had never even visited before that summer, with a one-year-old daughter and now the tragedy of losing our son, Jason. I remember riding back to our house to drop Laina off with fellow students as we prepared for Kerri to go through labor and delivery. She was so far along she had to move forward with the normal labor and delivery process, which is absolutely terrible when you know your child is dead. I remember driving back to the hospital while crying my eyes out and saying to God, "I knew at some point You were going to bring a great trial and test us, but I never dreamed it would be this great and in this way." I was sweating and weeping trying to find my way back to Richland Hospital from Columbia International University in the borrowed car we were driving, which had no air conditioning. I eventually made it to the hospital and the delivery was planned for the following morning. It was a tragic time, but once again Kerri displayed Divine strength.

To compound our current problems, we had very little money and no medical insurance. That was a real hurdle, but it wasn't front and center on this day. Kerri gave birth to Jason after hours of labor and they immediately took his little body and wrapped it in blankets and gave him to us. He was certainly big enough to be viable, with skin darkened from lack of blood flow, though you could clearly make out all of his features. All the staff members, these angels in scrubs, left us alone and we held him there for a while, crying and praying and mostly sitting close. Looking back, I was such an immature person at that time. I had no idea how much emotional strain this was putting on Kerri. She was going through all of this without her mother, without family support, and surely feeling all alone. Not only that, she had the burden of continuing to care for Laina immediately after this ordeal was over. The nurses came in and took pictures, made a clay impression of his little feet and put it all in a box for us. Then a nurse came in and asked if I was okay to have Jason's body cremated along with others and discarded.

I am not a huge fan of cremation to begin with, but there was no way I was going to have Jason cremated in something akin to a mass cremation. I asked what other options were available and she said I would have to reach out to a funeral home and talk with them about body transport, caskets, and burial if I wanted another option. I asked her how much something like that might cost and she said $1,000 minimum. I literally didn't have $1,000 to spend if Kerri and I were going to eat the rest of the summer. Not knowing what to do at the moment, that team of godly nurses came to our rescue. They called everywhere they could and finally found a family-run funeral home, Manigault-Hurley, that said they would provide complete burial services for Jason for $250 total. They owned a graveyard way out in the Northeast part of town where they did burials and had a special area just for infants. Here Jason could be buried in a small grave with a simple metal plate on the ground with his name. May God bless those people for their kindness to us when we were down at our lowest.

Days later, Jason was buried in Northeast Columbia. A great friend of mine, Scott Townsend, took a wooden axe handle, lacquered it, and burned Jason's name into it somehow. It was probably 12" tall. He cemented that cross into a plastic drinking cup so I could take it to the graveyard and plant it for Jason as a makeshift headstone. That wooden ax handle tombstone lasted for years and I will never forget Scott for his kindness in that dark moment. I will also never forget Jimmy, one of my Russian Language classmates that I had only known for only thirty days at that time. He came straight to our dorm as soon as he heard the news about Jason. I opened the door and he was standing there, already crying. He grabbed me and hugged me tight and that is when my violent crying came out. He never said a word, he didn't have to. He just came and hugged me in tears. When we finished crying, he said, "I love you, man," and he left. It was perfect. That is how you minister to people who have just gone through a tragic loss. You show up, you empathize, you hug them, and you let them know you love them and will do anything for them. That's it, nothing else is needed or required in those very holy and difficult moments because if you begin to talk too much, you will definitely say all the wrong things. I have used that interaction with Jimmy as a model for how I minister to folks in tragedy throughout my ministry career.

Looking forward, there were going to be many more painful moments over the next several years and we didn't have a clue they were coming. If we would have known, we probably wouldn't have gone. It would have been overwhelming to see what all that was coming our way. Not knowing, however, allowed us to keep moving forward step by step, day by day. I was excelling in learning Russian and Kerri was excelling in being a great mom. Just a few months later, we found out Kerri was pregnant once again. We were shocked and so was everyone else. Honestly, we didn't know if we should even tell our mission board for fear that they would tell us to stay home another year until Kerri gave birth, which would have been incredibly depressing. We did tell them, though, and she was early enough in her pregnancy that they cleared us to travel to Russia in mid-December 1998. We loaded up about eight large trunks full of Saran wrap, spices, chocolate chips, cooking utensils, peanut butter, and a million other American "necessities" before flying out of Grand Rapids airport on our way to Ufa, Russia. We just knew this was going to be our lifelong calling, working far away from home in a place with very few churches and even less Christian influence. Once again, we were mistaken, but it was going to be a very formative time in our lives, bringing wisdom and humility, as those two traits often travel together.

The simple grave marker made from an ax handle by my friend
Scott Townsend

CHAPTER 14

THIRD MISSIONARY JOURNEY

S imply arriving to our destination on our third missionary journey was difficult; completing it would require herculean endurance. We'd initially thought this third missionary journey would be to Pakistan or India, but at the last minute it was redirected by our seminary back to Central Asia. One of the Central Asian sites was located in Russia proper, so it was an easy choice for us to return to Russia. At this point, we assumed we would spend the rest of our lives there. Our other assumption was that the Russia we were returning to in 1999 would be the same Russia we had left at the end of 1995. Neither assumption turned out to be true.

During our second missionary journey, we had enjoyed good health, made great Russian friends, received a warm welcome everywhere we went, and experienced real fruit from our labor.

On our third missionary journey, we experienced almost none of the above. It was a time of trials and testing. In the end, we literally limped out of Russia on our way back home.

I had worked diligently on my Russian for the last six months and it was decent as I landed in Russia for this third missionary journey. Over the next two years it would get even better. Upon arrival, we were so relieved. We had been striving for this moment for three years and it had finally come. We were now employees of the International Mission Board of the Southern Baptist Convention, which provided us with medical benefits and a paycheck, things that had been beyond our reach for several years now. We were also in country with some of our very best friends, Sean and Kostanza Wentley. They had been our neighbors in seminary and had a beautiful daughter, Paula Joy, who was Laina's age. Right before we left, I reached out to Richland Memorial Hospital to set up a payment plan for our $2,800 hospital bill. The person I spoke with told me that they had written it off and I didn't owe them anything more. I am still not sure how this happened or who might have made it go away, and I didn't ask. I just said thanks and wrote them the best thank you card ever. In addition to that, my dear friend Scott Townsend paid our $1,700 hospital bill from Gadsden for us. I will never forget the kindness of all these people who blessed us along our journey.

Once again, we were arriving to Russia at the worst possible time, in the depth of winter. I went right to work securing for us necessary gear to survive a Russian winter. Fur-lined boots, coats, and shapkas, the classic Russian fur hat that is the most important piece of clothing since most of your body heat escapes from your head. Mine was easy to find at the local market, but Kerri needed a more stylish one, so that took some time. Keep in mind that most of this shopping is done outside at open-air markets when you don't have the clothes necessary to keep you warm! After securing the clothes that would allow us to survive during minus-forty-degree days, I went right to work on my Russian language skills, arising before dark to catch a bus that dropped me off about a half mile from my language coach's house. These early morning lessons were brutal as I was continuously corrected by my coach because I could barely roll my *R*s and could not make a guttural sound for one prominent Russian letter. Outside of that, I was doing pretty well and we were enjoying our new city and our friends.

After several months in the country, I realized there were approximately twenty-five missionaries from five different western countries in Ufa, a city of several million people. It was a nice enough place, but I had come all the way over here to get to that place where there were no missionaries. That place was Sibye, Russia, a small town barely larger than a village. In order to get to Sibye from Ufa, you had to endure a thirty-two-hour train ride, as there were no flights in and out of this small place even though there was a small airport occasionally utilized in the summer months. I decided we would move there and be "the tip of the spear" in starting Gospel work in that small town. I made all the plans I could and then traveled down myself, a few days before Kerri and Laina, so I could get everything set up for them.

I traveled on the train alone and some Russian friends from Ufa drove a truck down with our belongings. I arrived very early in the morning and we all spent a few hours setting up our flat. We had purchased a very soft, new couch and a lot of kitchen utensils, along with a decent bed and dresser. That was about it, as most Russian flats are rented furnished and don't have room for any new furniture. As I recall, we hired a few of the local boys from the courtyard to help us get the furniture into the house. They were in total awe of our new couch and bed, as most people in this town had not been able to even consider purchasing new furniture in decades with the economic chaos they were experiencing. According to our standards, we were traveling with minimal things, but to them it was very shocking to see so many new things, as families there were living on less than a hundred dollars a month.

The local group of guys couldn't stop talking about our stuff while we were moving it all into the apartment. I had a business visa and presented myself as an NGO humanitarian aid worker with a company our mission board had formed in the UK, Global SourceNet. What I didn't know was the Russian words for humanitarian aid workers were not familiar to these people way out in this small town so they didn't understand the verbiage. The concept of folks leaving one country to go and provide things for people in another country free of charge didn't fit into their worldview at all. That meant they thought our story was nothing but a ruse and we were probably either spies or some type of cult. After unloading everything and hearing this large group of guys talking incessantly about all of our nice things, I started to get nervous since all of them were drinking and one of them was already drunk.

Later in the day, after all my friends from Ufa had left to return home, this same guy came to my door and asked me for money. As one who had a brand new $300 couch and $500 bed, he knew I had money. I told him right away that I didn't give money to buy alcohol. I knew if I gave him money this first time it would start a precedent that would never end. He was drunk and not happy with my answer, but I stuck to it and eventually asked him if that was all, a polite way in Russian to say it is time for you to go. This particular guy was trouble, I could feel it and see it in his eyes, and he was the alpha male of this neighborhood clan. After I had gotten rid of him, I had this ominous feeling I was going to get visited later that night, as they knew I was totally alone and had money, lots of it!

I will never forget going to bed that night contemplating how I was going to respond if these guys forced their way into my flat, as they could have easily done. At that time, all I had was a simple wooden exterior door, not the usual steel door which was being installed in many flats for this very purpose. It was a common practice for thieves to break in and either beat you or lock you in a small toilet room and steal everything you had. I had a few thousand dollars with me, which I had hastily wrapped in aluminum foil and placed in the freezer to make it look like some type of food. I took out about $300 and was prepared to hand that over if I was met in the middle of the night by five or six drunken locals. As the night grew long, I was exhausted and desperately needed sleep, but the ominous feeling would not leave. I had slept very little the night before on the long train ride and it didn't feel like I was going to sleep this night either.

Before going to bed, I looked around the apartment for any type of weapon to defend myself. The best thing I could find was a claw hammer, which I put under my pillow. The last fight I was a part of was back in Gadsden when I was twenty years old and got jumped by two guys in a trailer. That night I'd fought one and then the other, and it didn't turn out well for me. I wrestled with the first guy before picking up a coat rack and swinging it at the second guy, only to have it shatter against his arm without him flinching. That is when I started using my words to talk my way out of that one before it got too bad. It only took a few stitches to the lip to fix me up after that fight. This night, however, I was hundreds of miles from any other missionary teammate with no real means of communication and these guys played by different rules. I was scared. Trying to go to sleep while frightened and sleeping on a claw hammer is not an easy feat, but I eventually pulled it off. Fortunately, I didn't have any visitors that night or the next while I was alone in Sibye. That made me feel like I had made my stand about handing out money for booze and I had made it past the danger zone of hostility. Now, I could welcome Kerri and Laina into this new place and feel a lot better about it.

As we settled into Sibye, our only contacts were a few nationals that were our friends and fellow believers, Renat and Aibulot. Outside of them, we were on an island. We had been there only a few weeks when I was summoned to the FSB (our CIA equivalent) headquarters and questioned by a 6'5", 260-pound behemoth of a man. It was an interrogation, as he was sure I was a CIA operative. I tried to convince him otherwise, but he never bought what I was selling. He tried to get me to drink vodka at ten a.m. to "loosen me up," but I was too smart to do that. He had other tactics as well. He would be friendly for ten minutes and ask about my family and education, then he would flip and get very stern for ten minutes, accusing me of all kinds of things from spying to insurrection. He alternated back and forth time and time again along with three others in the room for intimidation purposes. Following this "interview," a car followed us everywhere we went in Sibye, even though we were always walking since we didn't have a car.

We were living in a one-bedroom apartment of about seven-hundred square feet, so we put Laina in the single bedroom and often slept on that nice fold-out couch all the neighborhood guys so envied. Honestly, as time went on, we were tough and getting tougher. By this point, I was doing well with my Russian language by talking to all of the younger neighborhood boys in the courtyard, and we were making friends in our little apartment building. Things were going well until one day the boys in the courtyard showed me a notebook where they had handwritten all kinds of things. Looking through the pages, I could see that it was filled with pentagrams, drawings of demons, and crazy sexualized material. It was evil to the core and these were young teenage boys, all less than fifteen years of age. At that time, Sibye was that kind of a town, an evil place plagued by sexual violence and a syphilis epidemic.

Not only that, it was a violent place. One night Aibulot and I were walking home late in the pitch dark and were stopped by the local gang of hooligans, as they call them in Russian. They knew Aibulot and didn't really like him because he ran a camp for drug rehabilitation outside of town. When you do good things such as that in a dark place, it is convicting to the folks wallowing in evil and they often don't like you because of your light. Approximately eight of them surrounded us. I just knew we were going to get a beating. They cussed and threatened, but Aibulot was able to stay calm and somehow talk them out of it. I tried to look cool and confident while not saying a word during the ten-minute interaction, as they would have recognized my accent immediately and it would have really gotten ugly if they knew Aibulot had a foreigner with him, especially an American. We would have been robbed at a minimum, beaten at a maximum. It was a very dark place.

Outside of these threats, we almost had the most devastating loss a person could imagine. As a hyperactive two-year-old,

Laina had some older elementary-aged girls that thought the little American girl was absolutely adorable, so they would play with her in the courtyard under our watchful eye. She was already understanding Russian and English at this point because we only spoke English in our house and Russian outside. We threw her a birthday party for her second birthday on May 4, 2000, and these girls brought her pounds and pounds of Russian chocolate and goodies and this made them even closer. With all of that sweetness available on one single day, Laina did what any two-year-old would do—she ate until she threw up.

A few days later Laina was outside with one of the little girls who had befriended her. The girl was holding her hand and walking Laina around. The little girl was probably only nine or ten years old. Laina was a very strong-willed child so at some point, she decided she wanted to go somewhere different than where her newfound friend was leading her. Laina then pulled her hand away from the girl and the girl pulled back, but with Laina being a very strong-willed child, she pulled even harder and broke away. Once she had broken free, she started walking toward the swing set. If that doesn't sound frightening, it is because you have never seen a Russian swing set in Siberia.

The swing set frames in Russia are fabricated out of metal tubing and are approximately fourteen feet tall. The swings themselves are made by taking one half inch rebar and affixing it to the top of the swings and building a seat by welding this rebar to two-inch angle iron which forms a rectangular seat. The angle iron seat is usually about two feet long and eighteen inches deep. It is filled in with two-by-ten boards to form a solid seat surface. So the wood and steel that is swinging from a pulley fourteen feet in the air has to weigh fifty pounds before you even place a child on it and they most often swing with two children on each swing. Socialism didn't like for children to do anything alone so everything was built for at least two. This is in addition to the fact that when Russian kids swing, they always do it by standing on the steel and wooden seat, not sitting on it, as they can easily brace themselves with the stiff rebar from which the seat hangs. As you can see, it is set up to be a serious accident, and it was almost a catastrophic one for our two-year-old daughter.

As soon as Laina jerked away from her little Russian friend, I yelled for her and the entire playground froze as that fifty-pound swing came hurling down from its backswing ten feet up in the air, with about a ten-year-old child standing on the swing as it came down straight toward Laina's head. The child, as well as all of us, was helpless to stop it. The swing hurled down and missed Laina's head by no more than a centimeter, and that is generous. If it had hit her, it would have been the corner of the iron square seat right to her head. I have no doubt that it would have either killed her or left her severely deformed, probably blind in one eye at a minimum. Meanwhile, Laina was clueless, so she froze and looked at me wondering what was going on. That just meant that the swing has to pass by her head once more on the returning backswing. It barely missed her once again. At that point, the child on the swing jumped off and was able to hold on to the swing with others who ran it to catch it. My stomach literally hurts as I write these words because I am the only one who understands how close I came to losing Laina right there, in this faraway place thirty-two hours from any serious medical care. In this instance, God was merciful. Other health issues, however, would soon spring up and cause us to leave Sibye in a hurry, never to return.

As mentioned earlier, the Juvenile Rheumatoid Arthritis

(JRA) I thought would be gone forever had returned at age twenty-four. It then went back into remission while I was at seminary and had been a non-issue for several years by this time. Then, on the very day I moved to Sibye, my knees began to swell once again. This was not random chance, this was spiritual warfare. My knees stayed swollen and painful for years following this reoccurrence. The things I am about to write will seem very strange to some, but my experience in this is real. Sibye was a spiritually dark place, full of rape, prostitution, epidemic STDs, pornography, demonic symbols such as those the young children were drawing in my courtyard, and addiction of all kinds. It was a place where God had been set aside for decades, and when God is set aside the angel of light, also known as the devil, fills the gap. He fills it subtly and masks his intentions, but at the end of the day he is the father of lies who wants to bring death and destruction to God's beloved creation, mankind. Thus, when people refuse to worship or even acknowledge God, Satan has free reign to work out his evil intentions, and he does horrible things when he is given free reign.

This was happening in Sibye in 1999. As a matter of fact, the spiritual darkness was so tangible there you could literally feel it. I well remember my friend, Sean Wentley, coming down from Ufa to check on us after about four or five weeks since we'd been out there all alone. After just a few hours, he said, "Todd, it is so dark and oppressive here, I can feel it. Do you feel that?" Others had told us the same thing when they came to visit. Sean affirmed that even in Ufa it didn't feel like this, as the feeling of darkness lifted as soon as he left Sibye. We certainly felt it at times, but when you live there you adjust and forget how you felt it so prominently when you first arrived. It was probably a lot of what I felt that first night there, frightened and with a two-year JRA remission destroyed.

Looking back at those ten weeks in Sibye, I realize that in this very small amount of time I had suffered a major flare-up of my arthritis, Laina was almost killed on a playground, Aibulot and I were almost beaten down by a group of hooligans, and at the very end, Kerri went into premature labor at six months. When you load up and drive deep into the darkness, there will be real pain and resistance, and so it was with us. When Kerri's early contractions started, we feared the worst after having just buried Jason less than a year earlier. I attempted to find any medical help in the city, but there was very little available. I remember the one place we went where we thought we might get help, they wanted to give Kerri electric stem treatments in her calves to control her preterm labor. I am not an obstetrician, but I was pretty sure that was not going to work. That's when I knew I had to get us out of there as fast as possible, but you can't get out of Sibye quickly. I immediately went into emergency mode. I called our friends in Ufa and they secured for us airline tickets to get from Ufa to Limassol, Cyprus, a city on the island where there was western medical care available and a safe house maintained by our mission board where we could live for a few months. First, though, we had to actually get there before we lost another child!

I honestly don't remember the train ride from Sibye back to Ufa, but thirty-two hours in an 8' x 8' cabin with a sick wife and a two-year-old is not a fun trip. We arrived to Ufa and our mission board told us what type of prescription medicine Kerri should take, but of course we had to try to translate or transliterate that complex prescription name into Russian or German to even know what to look for in the local pharmacies. And of course, the medicine was nowhere to be found in any pharmacy in Ufa, but our friends found some in a city eight hours away, the city of Kazan. They bought it and paid a taxi driver $100 to drive it down to us and told him they would give him another $100 if he succeeded in his mission and returned. We were probably only 50 percent certain this was the appropriate medicine, but we were desperate. Plus, even if it was the right medicine, we were only 50 percent sure what was in the bottle was what it said on the label. There was no FDA in Russia at that time and medicines were imported from Germany, Italy, France, etc., so there was lots of room for fraud.

Kerri started taking the medicine once we arrived in Ufa, and the following day we made the three-hour flight to Moscow, where we stayed the night with other missionaries since we couldn't get a direct flight to Cyprus. The next day, we made it to Cyprus, four full days after Kerri's contractions had begun. Immediately upon arrival, we took Kerri to the birthing clinic of Dr. Marios Liasedes, a name I will always remember. He was a guy that looked like Mark Anthony, with thick wavy hair and perfect olive skin. He wore white pants and a simple white T-shirt and spoke very slowly and kindly. As soon as he evaluated her, she was admitted and he gave her some injections to help develop the lungs of our child. At the time, we had no idea she would be there for the next three weeks while Laina and I learned to live in Cyprus, a former British colony in the Mediterranean. Some of the skills we had to master quickly were driving on the left side of the road instead of the right, learning to drive a stick shift with your right hand doing the gear shifting and learning all about roundabouts. That, along with battling a never-ending fight with no-see-ums and Mediterranean heat. Thankfully, we found a very beautiful oasis only a few miles away from our home—a McDonald's! Laina and I medicated ourselves throughout the transition with lots of ice cream cones.

Kerri, on the other hand, was stuck in Dr. Liasedes's birthing clinic, trying to hold on until she reached thirty-six weeks so that the baby would have sufficient time to develop her lungs. This is yet another reminder of how strong and courageous Kerri is and how she has proven that time and time again throughout our married life.

We would visit her every day for a few hours, as poor Kerri was bored to death. She would be given Greek yogurt with honey every evening for dinner and she hated it, so I would eat it for her while Laina climbed through the cabinets in her room at the clinic. That is also when Kerri started reading fiction and I took her every good book I could find on the island. Meanwhile, I was trying to teach Laina to sleep in a "big girl bed" back at home.

I had found a rheumatologist on the island who had drained my knees for me, but the relief was short-lived. I still remember trying to get in and out of the small Honda car we were using at the time. I couldn't bend my leg more than about thirty degrees, so it was quite a feat to fold my six-foot frame into that tiny car with one leg almost straight the entire time. Then, to add insult to injury, I awoke one morning with a terrible pain in my groin area. I had experienced kidney stones in college and thought that might be the problem because of the intensity of the pain. I called a missionary colleague and asked if she could take me to the local clinic to see what was going on while another missionary colleague watched Laina. A Cypriot physician, who was German-trained, evaluated me and told me very nonchalantly that I had a testicular torsion.

"A testicular what?!" I replied. "What does that mean, what do we do for that?"

"We will need to go to the hospital right away and do a surgery to correct it. I will cut open your scrotum, take your testicle, twist it, then sew it back into place," he said very casually.

"Wait, wait, I'm not sure about driving straight over to the hospital and having my scrotum cut open based on a five-minute evaluation, Doc! What are my other options?"

"None. If you don't do it your testicle will die within four hours or less for lack of blood flow because of the torsion," he said very matter-of-factly in his accented English.

"Okay, Doc, you convinced me, let's do it ASAP!"

What was so surreal is he calmly gave me directions to the hospital from his office and said he would meet me there. I guess he canceled his book of business for the day. My colleague who had taken me to the appointment drove me to the hospital and dropped me off, as she had to return and take care of Laina. Sleeping all alone in Sibye with that hammer was frightening, but walking into this hospital in Cyprus all alone and wondering about the skill level of the physicians who were about to cut my manhood open was even more so. I called Kerri at the birthing clinic and told her I was about to have a surgery for some freak issue I had never heard of before and Laina was with Bonnie for a few days. Literally, the very next thing I remember is an Indian doctor putting a mask over my face and me having a million doubts in my mind about if this was the right thing and how it was going to work out.

When I woke up the following day, I tried to get up and that was a major mistake. I immediately realized that on a scale of one to ten, I had a pain level of twelve. I think I was in the hospital for three days, but I was still in horrific pain when I returned home. The comical part is Kerri and I were released right at the same time, so we both went from the hospital to our bedroom in Cyprus and were pinned to the bed. I was recovering and she was on bedrest. The part that was not funny was we had a hyperactive two-year-old daughter and both of us were bedridden, helpless to care for her. Fortunately, one of our fellow missionaries, Bonnie Johnson, was gracious enough to move in with us for several days or maybe even a week to cook for us and keep Laina entertained, as we didn't have any other option.

Circumstances such as this are part of the difficulty and beauty of missionary life. You have this larger missionary community and you are so interdependent with each other. Things like this happen pretty frequently and one of your colleagues has to step up, just as your family would back at home, and take care of you in very close quarters, like moving into your home for a season. It is a special community with real love and compassion for one another. After a week or so, I was finally able to start moving around and soon thereafter, Kerri was finally released from her bedrest as she approached her ninth month. We had pierced the darkness for just a few months in Sibye and we had paid a high price for it. Even so, we were still putting one foot in front of the other through the love and support of our missionary family.

On July 25, 2001, Amanda Sheryl Carnes made her grand entrance into the world as a happy, healthy baby girl. We were thrilled and it finally seemed as though things might get back to some form of normal. We remained in Cyprus for six weeks with our newborn, per our mission board's policy, and then made our way back into Russia with our two little girls.

On our way back to Ufa from Cyprus, we hit yet another crisis, a crisis Kerri and I will never forget. It is funny now, but it wasn't then. While attempting to fly to Ufa from Moscow's domestic "Domadyedova" airport, we literally ran out of money. I mean, we didn't have a cent to our name. Cyprus has strict currency laws due to all of the mafia money laundered in their banks, so we could not access our funds before starting our journey back into Russia. That being the case, all I could do was gather all the cash I could and try to get back to Russia on a razor-thin budget. We were doing fine until our last cab ride between airports in Moscow, as there was a required one-hour taxi ride from the Moscow International Airport to the domestic airport. That trip cost more than I had expected and I had come up about twenty dollars short of what we needed to pay for our overweight baggage.

Initially, I thought it wasn't a big deal and told the airport cashier to just keep my final bag and send it later. That way we could travel on to Ufa with the bags that were allowed and I would just replace those items if they never showed up, which was probable. Unfortunately, that is not how they wanted to do it. She told me in no uncertain terms that without the twenty dollars we could not board the plane at all, as she could not just keep the bag and allow us to board. Not only that, but I was talking to this lady through one of those little holes in the glass in a dimly lit area, so it was really hard to converse. I do remember her somewhat mocking me to her colleagues by saying, "Amercanyets bez deneg," which means, "Look at this American without any money?!" As our final words, she told me there was absolutely nothing she could do to help me and I needed to get out of the way so she could help others. At that moment, I literally looked around and thought, "I am going to have to beg. I need to start asking these people around me for a few rubles here and there and beg for the money we need to go home." I had to think fast as the plane was already boarding and if it departed, I was going to be stuck in a dirty, dimly lit Moscow airport with my two daughters, one a newborn, with no money and no contact info for any of the missionaries who lived in Moscow. What would I do if that happened? I was going to beg or rob or do whatever was necessary to avoid that catastrophe.

At that very moment, just seconds before I started to beg from strangers, I had a brainstorm. Russia can be a very harsh place in a public venue such as this, which means cashiers behind a counter generally could care less about you or your problems. They have a very tough job and at this time in their history, customer service was not a recognized concept. One thing they do always care about, however, is children, especially infants. It is an integral part of their culture. Infants always come first no matter the circumstances. Moms with infants go to the front of every line without question. It is actually a beautiful and redemptive part of their culture that we often miss here in America, where infants can be seen as a nuisance.

I had already explained to this lady that I had a two-year-old and an infant with me, but she had not seen them for herself. Kerri was seated with both of them about thirty yards away trying to care for them amid all the stress. At that point, I had no choice but to go and grab Kerri and both girls, leaving our bags where they lay to be stolen or whatever, in order to bring Kerri and the girls to the dimly lit window where this lady was telling me there was absolutely nothing she could do. I approached the counter in front of everyone and demonstrably said, "Look, I have my six-week old infant and no money and no supplies! I must get to Ufa or we will not have food for her, or even a place to sleep tonight. Please, the bag is an extra $20, my friends will pay you $100 when I land in Ufa." Culturally, I had pushed her over the edge. Once she actually laid eyes on little six-week-old Amanda, she literally called on the radio and stopped the Aeroflot jet on the runway! We were immediately driven out to the jet by an airport security car. The captain dropped the steps on the runway and we climbed in, only to be stared at with disdain by all the other passengers who were very annoyed the jet was being delayed for us "foreigners." When we made it back to Ufa, they took $150 off of my friends, but I didn't care. I would have paid $1,000 just to get back to the safety of home and get Amanda into a warm place to sleep, as it was September already.

Upon our return, we were introduced to our new home, a two-bedroom flat in the "Karablee Dom," or the "ship house." It had that name because it was the largest apartment building in the city. We were also introduced to the biggest Godsend ever, a young Tatar lady named Lilya Trussova. She would become our nanny and help us survive with two small children and no family support. We all loved Lilya dearly and she became like family. She loved our children so well and took care of us in every way. At the time, she was no more than twenty years old. She especially loved Amanda because she had been pregnant and lost a child who would have been about Amanda's age, so she loved and cared for her especially well. I think it was actually healing for her to have this experience.

We introduced Lilya to all kinds of American items. Her favorite was definitely brownies. In return, she kept us in the know about Russian culture so that we didn't make nearly as many cultural faux pas, such as the one I made in the supermarket when I was coming in and they asked me to put my bag in a holder against the wall so that I wouldn't steal anything. I didn't understand their request at first, but then caught on. On the way out, I intended to tell the ladies working there that I was mistaken about the bag earlier, but the words for "I was mistaken" and "I am a mistake" are very similar. Of course I told them, "I am a mistake," and they burst out laughing. I didn't know what was so funny until I arrived home to explain it to Lilya, who also died laughing. We had many good laughs at my expense.

The first snows always arrive in early October in that part of Russia, so winter was about to bear down on us. As you can imagine, we were physically and emotionally exhausted from all the pain and trials of the last six months. Now, it was time to face down a long Russian winter with an infant and a toddler in a tiny flat. When the high temps are minus ten degrees and the lows are minus thirty degrees, you can go outside if you are dressed to the hilt with fur and layers, but your small children can only be transported from apartment to car on most days, with maybe five minutes outside to play. That makes winters miserable. What's worse, winter also brings with it very short days, with daylight hours of no more than seven hours in the middle of winter, about ten a.m. until five p.m.

This last winter in Russia definitely had some high points, but mixed in were some real lows as well. The primary low was the debilitating swelling of my knee joints with my continuing flare of arthritis. I was bedridden for days at a time with painfully swollen knees such that my legs would hardly bend. This is a nightmare in a Russian winter, as the tiny elevators often quit working so you are left to climb several flights of stairs to go in and out of your apartment building. To alleviate the pain, a Russian friend located for me an orthopedic doctor in Ufa. I made my way to his office one day, where I discovered at least fifty people waiting, all standing in a cramped space with no seating. What happened next made me feel very uncomfortable. Someone came out and took me by the hand and led me into his office ahead of everyone else who had already been there for quite some time, most of them elderly. That is just the way it is in Russia. There are those who have to wait in lines and those who don't, and foreigners were generally pressed to the front. We have that same thing in America, but there is a difference between the two systems. In America, this inequality is hidden out of necessity. In Russia, it happens overtly and everyone is unapologetic about it. It is what it is in their culture.

The physician immediately began to explain that he could drain my knee for me and inject it with cortisone (I will never forget the name of the cortisone, Kenalog-40), but I would have to stay in the hospital for three days for monitoring. This mentality of going to the hospital for long periods of time for almost anything is quite the norm in Russia, but I wasn't buying it. I had seen my knees drained in as little as fifteen minutes in physician's offices many times. This is where the argument began. I tried to politely let him know that I was not going to check into a hospital to be "observed" after having a knee drained. He then said he wouldn't drain it. I reached for my bag of supplies and said I would go find another physician in town who would take care of me, a total bluff since I had no other option. The bluff worked, however, and he agreed to do the aspiration procedure and let me go home because he really wanted to be the one to treat the American.

I had this procedure performed five or six times over the next several months. The occurrence that stands out most prominently in my memory is when I went alone. I flagged a cab and went to the pharmacy to buy the disposable needles and Kenalog-40. I then proceeded to the hospital and began to stand in line, as I couldn't bear to place myself in front of all of these poor people who had no recourse. I think I stood there for about an hour in pain when a nurse suddenly recognized me at the rear and brought me back to the exam room. The exam rooms were definitely something from the 1950s, with old lights that didn't work and ancient exam tables. Also, they didn't have any disposable implements at that time. Everything they used was either glass or metal, including the large vials of injectable medicines.

About that time, the doctor came in and immediately asked why I had not just come to the front instead of waiting with the others. I explained that it wasn't comfortable for me to break into the front of the line. He fussed about that and then laid me on the antique examination table and left. As they were preparing for the procedure this time, there was suddenly a flurry of activity with people running around frantically. Then a nurse came in and asked sheepishly, "Would you like to use Novocain?"

"Absolutely!" I answered.

At that point, she didn't reply to me and I realized what was happening. Culturally, it was shameful for them to admit that they didn't have any Novocain available, so she asked if I wanted to use Novocain without overtly admitting they didn't have any available. I was supposed to pick up on this cultural cue and not force her to say it, but rather make up some excuse to go and get it myself.

Figuring all of this out in a few seconds, I jumped in with, "Listen, let me go to a pharmacy nearby and pick up some Novocain, as I am embarrassed to always use yours since I know you need it for all your other patients. I meant to bring it with me this time anyway. I will be right back!" With that, I took off to flag another cab and get some Novocain, a lot of it!

I wanted to leave a large amount with them for others, as I well-remembered having my knees drained as a child and I swear they didn't use any Novocain at that time. I didn't want anyone to experience this and I am sure it was still happening, as I have heard some real horror stories from others about Soviet era hospitals. I spoke to a Russian friend who had his ruptured appendix removed with only localized anesthesia because his operation was happening on the day of a large parade and there was no one available to put him to sleep. He said it was so painful they tied him to the bed to keep him still. Eventually, he passed out from the pain. There were other stories of tonsillectomies and the removal of adenoids in children without putting them to sleep, just strapping their heads onto the bed. Medicine was often barbaric even in the 1980s and '90s in the former Soviet Union. As for me, each injection generally brought with it approximately a month of relief, and then the process started over.

The physical pain of ailments such as my JRA are difficult to bear, but the pain itself is not nearly as traumatizing as the mental and emotional anguish it brings with it. It is one thing to have swollen, stiff, and painful knees while lying in a bed all day, but what is worse is the dark projections into the future that run through your mind while you lie there. "Will I ever get over this? What if I don't? Will I be permanently disabled? What if this jumps from my knees to my arms or my spine? Will I be a person who is homebound and can't provide for my family while eating pain pills to survive?" These are the real questions that torment the soul as you lie there alone with only your thoughts and anxieties, wishing you could get up and play with your children. This ailment made this time in my life, and indeed in my entire family's life, very difficult for all.

However, there was an upside in that it very clearly taught me about the true emotional pain that always accompanies chronic disease. Unless you have lain in a bed alone and wrestled with these thoughts for days and weeks at a time, along with severe pain, you can never fully understand how the real pain of chronic disease is the constant threat of it crippling or killing you and destroying your future. The real pain is the lack of control you feel as you realize you have no recourse against its desired path in your body. The disease is the master and you are the slave. You feel powerless, knowing it will do whatever it wills. This is both frightening and exhausting, especially when you have real responsibilities as a husband and father. Through this season of life, I struggled mightily, but this experience certainly taught me how to empathize with others. Ultimately, God was merciful and delivered me from the debilitating symptoms of this disease many years later through a new class of biologic treatments, though the arthritis is still a constant threat in my life to this very day.

Apart from the trials of this season, there is one phenomenal story that must be told. This is one of those stories you can't wait to see from the lens of heaven since there were so many things you never saw to completion. The story begins in a very remote village named Keezgee, a very typical village of approximately two to three hundred people. It was located approximately three hours by car from our city of Ufa and through a series of random events we began to visit there. After a few visits, we were able to show them the Jesus film in their native language, Bashkir, and in this way began to teach them about Jesus. They were cultural Muslims by tradition, but in reality they were not really knowledgeable of what Islam even meant. I remember one older gentleman telling me right away how he remembered his country saying God is a fairy tale and how he believed them, losing his entire life to this lie. He was so remorseful about it as he described it to me. I tried to explain to him that as long as there is life there is time for forgiveness, but he could never believe that God's grace was gracious enough to forgive him after he proclaimed God to be dead for decades of his life. That very story is a sad tale I saw over and over again during my three years in the former Soviet Union.

With a few receptive people in this village, we began to visit more often, driving three hours each way to spend two to three hours in the village. We would always stop about fifty miles outside of town at the last available store to buy several lengths of Russian sausage, called *kolbasa*. They had very little meat in their normal diet and suffered greatly from this lack of protein. We were eager to help them with this as long as it was in a way that didn't embarrass or demean them. In order to do that, we would always ask them to make fresh bread and tea and we would supply the fresh sausage. With each visit, we would sit around their home and eat together while talking about eternal things. I even took Laina once and we rode one of their horses while we ate the meat of another horse they had just killed. As is often the case, the most receptive family was on the lower end of the economic and power system of the village, which made them very vulnerable. That made befriending outsiders very risky for them, but they were brave and kind, and always received us warmly.

Eventually, we were invited to put on a public presentation of the Jesus film in Bashkir for the entire community. About twenty people came out that day to the tiny meeting hall where they had community meetings. After the film, we had a few people share some testimonies, including Sean Wentley's Greek father-in-law, Nikos. Nikos's age demanded some respect in their eastern culture, so he was well-received. It was a memorable experience because Nikos could only speak in Greek, so Sean would translate from Greek to English, I would translate from English to Russian, and Fareet would translate from Russian to Bashkir.

We all felt like it went well, so we were looking forward to building upon this early foothold within this village to continue bringing people toward the Gospel. We were even more encouraged when Rezeda, the mother of our primary family in the village, recounted to us one of her dreams. She told us that after we showed them the Jesus film in Bashkir, Jesus had come to her in a vision at night and he spoke to her in her native language, Bashkir. She was astounded to hear this because she thought of Jesus as the Russian's God and he should only speak Russian, not Bashkir! That night Jesus told her we were from Him and the books we provided were His words. It was amazing for her and for us. Through this special vision, she became convinced that the things we were presenting were real and the One, True God was speaking to her through us, these clumsy foreigners. Our hopes were high for this entire village, but the realities of spiritual warfare were about to press back upon us.

Following our public presentation, we returned about a week later and Rezeda caught us before we went very far in the village, as her house was situated on the outskirts. She immediately began to explain what had happed in the last week. The leader of the village, a lady for whom Rezeda worked by milking her cows, had begun to spread rumors about us. She was telling everyone that we were the "Belaya Bratya," the "White Brothers," a gang within Russia. The gang was well-known as a violent, Nazi-style cult. The village leader told everyone we were affiliated with these White Brothers and we were there only to make inroads so that we could kill their sons and kidnap their daughters. This was ludicrous, of course, but in these small rural areas totally cut off from civilization it is not very difficult for a fantastical rumor like this to get started. Once started by anyone of standing in the community, it is almost impossible to disprove.

Before we were able to return, this village leader had already come to Rezeda and told her that she was not to host us in this village anymore since we were such a dangerous threat. Rezeda, the poor lady with no power or recourse, stood firm with us against her village leader, a very dangerous move. As a result, the village leader fired her from her job of milking cows and basically excommunicated her from the village.

As Rezeda recounted all of this to me, I was speechless and heartbroken. We were standing in her two-room wooden home, the type of wooden home where you can see straight through the boards to the ground, which made it always bitterly cold. The reality of what had just happened to her hit me like a ton of bricks. I knew I was going to get in my Toyota 4Runner and drive back to my home in Ufa in a few hours, safe from any physical or financial repercussions in this village. Rezeda, on the other hand, had no such recourse. She had been born and raised in this village. Life here had not been kind to her before she met us, and now I felt this wave of guilt, wishing I would have never come to her house because I was so frightened by how her physical future was going to impacted by this crazy turn of events. Her loyalty to us, foreigners she barely knew, had now brought about real-life repercussions for her and her family.

Overcome with emotion, I began to apologize profusely to her and her family in Russian, which they mostly understood. "Rezeda, I am so sorry. I never meant for this to happen to you or your family. You all are so kind and warm and we only wanted to bring good to you, not harm. Is there anything at all I can possibly do to help? Can I go talk to the village leader? I am so sorry!"

I will never in my life forget her very profound response. "Anton, Bogshe yest!" In English that is translated as "Anthony, God exists!" (I went by my first name, Anthony, in Russia because they couldn't pronounce Todd.)

I was so heartbroken as I thought of all she and her family might lose in the years and decades to come, yet here she was comforting me, the one who had lost nothing, by reminding me of God's eternal power. I was broken. I was humbled. I felt ashamed and relieved at the same time. Ashamed that my faith was so small in comparison to hers, relieved that God had obviously really come to her in that dream and provided her with a measure of faith that caused her to not care what folks in the village thought of her or how they might treat her. I'll never forget it.

I don't know how things ultimately worked out for Rezeda and her family because something new and different was about to happen in Ufa that would seal us off from them forevermore. Nevertheless, I had once again been clearly taught that many who are first shall be last, and many who are last shall be first. God had not chosen the village leaders, the village bankers, or the strongmen of the village to hear His word and receive it through a supernatural vision. He had chosen the very simple, humble Rezeda, a poor woman on the very fringes of society even in her tiny Siberian village. Ironically, she was very similar to my own grandmother, Mama White, who used to iron clothes for other mill workers in the mill village, but she milked cows for the other villagers in Keezgee, Russia. She was kind and open and just the type of person God most often seems to choose when looking to plant His words in a new place.

Experiences such as this are one reason I can so easily get frustrated with the American church. As Americans, we are in love with star power. Everybody is chasing their fifteen minutes of fame on TikTok or Instagram and is willing to do about anything to obtain it. Furthermore, we stand in awe of athletes, entertainers, models, and others, many of whom very obviously stand in awe of themselves. We follow their every move, seek them out just to "get close" to them and grab a selfie with them in the background, a great boasting point for our own social media alter ego. We love star power. God, on the hand, loves most everything that is in direct contradiction to star power. He loves humility and hates pride. He loves thanksgiving and hates self-congratulatory exaltation. He loves the deference of teamwork and despises arrogant individualism. He very forthrightly says that He is the God of the poor and not the God of the rich, a generalized statement showing He aligns Himself with the oppressed, not the oppressors. But let any famous chest-thumping athlete or entertainer suddenly make an unproven verbal proclamation of allegiance to Jesus and American churches will immediately crown them as Pastor, Pope, and Evangelist extraordinaire within days.

Every time this happens, and it happens a lot, we are assuming the Kingdom of God works exactly like the kingdom of man. We assume star power is finally going to legitimize the Gospel to millions who adore the rich and famous yet are apathetic toward Jesus. As a believer, it is always embarrassing to watch this happen again and again because the Kingdom of God doesn't work any-thing like the kingdom of man. God is not impressed with star power, nor does He even prefer it. He likes to take the foolish things of this world and use them to confound the wise.

As I often told my church, the Gospel does not need celebrity endorsement. In fact, celebrity endorsement is often a hindrance to the Gospel because people devalue the Gospel when they fool-ishly think it is going to somehow be "empowered" by a celebrity. God is impressed with those who have proven their allegiance to His Kingdom over time, not those who have risen to fame in con-tradiction to his values. When we reduce the Kingdom of God to a "brand" that is going to benefit from celebrity endorsement, we truly show our own ignorance of who God is and how He oper-ates. When he saved the notorious Saul of Tarsus in order to use him mightily in the first century church, he didn't leverage Saul's "star power." Rather, the first thing he did was send him off to the desert for more than a decade to destroy his ego and fame in order to teach him that the Gospel alone, not his resume or name recognition, would be his strength. We would do well to remind ourselves of the same as the world laughs at our infatuation with fame in obvious contradiction to Jesus and his teachings.

Back in Ufa, the heat on our team was continuing to ratchet up during this time as Russian nationalism was being pressed to the fore. The country was in such chaos from the violence and extortion of the Russian mafia and random gangs that the Russian people did the unthinkable and elected a former KGB agent, Vladimir Putin, to the presidency. Electing someone this radical would have been inconceivable even four years previously, but the dire economic situation alongside the Russian Mafia's domination had made the people desperate for a strong leader who could put things back in order. Putin was the guy they felt could accomplish that, and he did. The problem is that leaders who are this strong never go away, as evidenced by the fact that Putin is now in year twenty of his rule although they have a constitutional presidential term limit of twelve years.

With Putin's ascendance to the presidency, he immediately began with his nationalistic agenda, part of which was to remove as many foreigners as possible from the country. Our team, along with others, found ourselves in the bull's-eye. With a little digging around, they discovered that we were making trips out to the villages. Even more damning, they discovered we were funding the translation of the New Testament into Bashkir. They did not approve of this type of religious meddling. In their worldview, the Russian people are Orthodox Christians, the Bashkir people are Muslims, and there is no reason for anyone to ever cross from one side to the other. They believe you are born into one religion or the other and it is primarily an ethnic marker as opposed to an individual belief system concerning God and eternal life.

These things, along with the fact that our team leader was an army veteran, were more than enough evidence for them to label us as "American spies" and summarily expel us from the country. After a full day of interrogations, they simply canceled our visas and told us we had five days to leave the country or we would be imprisoned. Being the overconfident Americans that we were, we immediately called the American Consulate in Ekaterinburg and told them the situation, asking if they could really do that to us. The consulate workers had just the right reply for us: "This is Russia and they can do whatever they want. Get your stuff and get out of here. Make sure you fly out of Moscow on the fourth day, not the fifth, just in case your flight gets canceled, because if you are here on the sixth day regardless of circumstances, you are going to prison and we will not be able to help you." Those were clear orders even overzealous Americans could clearly understand. We immediately purchased tickets from Ufa to Moscow and then on to Limassol, Cyprus, Amanda's birthplace. Now all we had to do was sell two apartments, three cars, and all the furnishings from five leased apartments in seventy-two hours. FIRE SALE!

When the dust settled from all the transactions, we had about $250,000 in cash, mostly Russian rubles, in a large sack. The plan was to transport that cash to Moscow and make it look like anything but money. The average wage at this time was about $2,000 per year, so translated to American dollars in 2020, it would be like having a large vinyl bag with $4 million inside. With no way to get that kind of money across a border, we had to get it to Moscow to spread out among our missionary colleagues there, who could then slowly get it out of the country over time. If the mafia had discovered we had that kind of money, we would have disappeared into the Siberian snow for sure. Somehow, though, we made it to Moscow and then on to Cyprus.

In the midst of the fire sale, we were also forced into very hasty goodbyes with all of our dear friends. I hardly slept at all with all the adrenaline coursing through my body. I remember we had one last Sunday in this three-day window and we went to church to see our friends. While I was there, a young Russian lady came up to me and asked if I thought she had sinned by voting for Putin. I went into political mode and dodged the question, as I had no energy for that type of discussion while we were under such pressure. It has always stood out in my mind, though, how she voted for him and within days felt frightened about what she had done. I think that was the reaction of most of the citizens at that time.

Upon returning home from church that final day, I discovered that our landlord had come to our apartment and entered, probably taking stock of what all was there for fire sale pricing since we were leaving. In Russia at that time, it wasn't unusual for your landlord to come into your house unannounced and look around. On this day, however, she made a mistake. When we tried to enter we found that she had not only locked the exterior steel door, which had been installed for safety from break-ins, she had also locked the original wooden door which was within, just behind the steel door. I never locked the original wooden door, as my thought process was if you get through this solid steel door that weighs two hundred pounds, the wood door is not going to help. That also meant that I never carried keys for the three different dead bolt–type locks that were on the wooden door. So we found ourselves stressed, full of adrenaline, and locked out of our own apartment with only one day to get out of the country. What was even worse, we were standing in a stinking foyer with Kerri holding Amanda and Laina, both of whom were cold.

Suddenly, I snapped. I grabbed the doorknob of the wooden door and thrust my shoulder into it. Nothing happened, so I did it again. I hit it a third time and I heard some wood begin to faintly crack. That sound was like the smell of blood to a great white shark. I started throwing my shoulder into the door again and again, harder and harder as more and more wood snapped and popped until the entire lock side of the door broke into pieces and opened. I looked behind me and saw Kerri, Laina, and our driver, Oleg, a former mafia member himself, staring at me big eyed. Oleg said, "Da tee shto!" which is loosely translated as "Wow!" The very next day we were off and on our way to Cyprus, a day early as advised.

As we left Ufa, I was sad, but also relieved. I had spent more than a year sick, depressed, often bedridden, caring for my wife as much as possible since her role was twice as difficult as mine. In the midst of it all, there was no way I could continue on much longer with my knees as they were, barely able to walk at times in a place where you walked most places. Also, buying black market Novocain and cortisone every six weeks was not sustainable. This meant that even before Putin rose to power and expelled our entire team from the county, I'd known we couldn't stay. I was hobbled, discouraged, and wondering if all the sacrifice was even worth it. The one great victory we had was certainly going to carry a very high price tag for Rezeda and her family, and all the other places where we might have had an impact were probably going to similarly write us off as a foreign cult focused on kidnapping their daughters. That is a very far cry from being a sacrificial Christian missionary society there to help them physically as well as spiritually, but the truth doesn't always win out in this world, at least with the majority.

Kerri was physically healthy, but she had been put through a season of testing that would have destroyed the mental and physical health of most anyone. She miscarried in Columbia, South Carolina, and buried her son all alone in a nondescript grave without a service or even a marker. She then moved 15,000 miles from home only to spend 90 percent of her time locked behind the walls of a tiny flat with a toddler and very little time for language acquisition. Following this was the spiritual onslaught of an incredibly tenuous emergency medical extraction to Cyprus, consummated with a long three-week stay in a Cypriot clinic away from her husband and daughter. When Amanda was finally born healthy, that was a great relief for us all, but upon returning to Russia Kerri was locked down in our apartment during those seven-hour days and seventeen-hour nights for months on end. Often, I was either bedridden with joints so swollen I could barely walk, or out in the villages and other places trying to make a difference during the times of relief following the injections. To endure all of that, she again proved herself to be one of the strongest people I know, but it was obvious that she was exhausted, depressed, and lonely. Even so, she never once said she was ready to quit and go home. She was willing to stay the course and finish our term until we were expelled by the government four months early. When I think of mentally tough people, she is the toughest I have ever known.

Rezeda (second from left) in her home in Keezgee

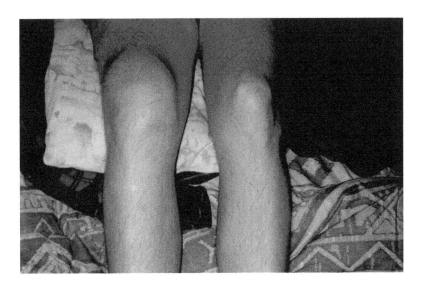

*The crippling swelling my arthritis caused during our third mis-
sionary journey*

PART THREE:

FINISHING WELL

Where there is no vision, the people perish: but he that keepeth the law, happy is he.

—Proverbs 29:18 (KJV)

I find the farther that I climb
    There's always another line of mountaintops
    It's never gonna stop
And the more of anything I do
    The thing that always ends up true
    Is getting what I want will never be enough

So I just want to look more like love
I just want to look more like love
This whole world is spinning crazy
    And I can't quite keep up
It's the one thing around here
    We don't have quite enough of
So I just want to look a little more like love
I just want to look more like love

Ben Rector, *More Like Love*

CHAPTER 15

RESURRECT THE
VISION!

After a quick one week debrief in Cyprus, we found ourselves back in Michigan, living in the basement of Kerri's parent's home. Life had been a complete whirlwind for so long, a place that was familiar to us was nice. I think we had about $15,000 or so when we landed in the US, with two or three months of medical insurance to be provided by the mission board. A family friend's mother had just passed away and her home was still fully furnished. When she heard about our situation, she offered to rent this place to us while we figured out what was next. As for what was next, I had no clue.

I hit the ground running as usual, and started doing some painting on the house we were leasing in exchange for paying rent to save our money. We took $6,500 in cash and bought a 1994 green Dodge Caravan. Yes, it was ugly, but it got the job done and it was a thousand times better than our Russian Niva Jeep. In addition to this, I began to work with my sister-in-law's company, stocking some grocery store shelves late at night to pick up some extra cash.

I grew up working hard and have never shied away from it. I do, however, remember how humbling it was to be there with my civil engineering degree plus a Master's in Biblical languages and find myself stocking shelves alongside a seventeen-year-old junior in high school. After several months of this, I found myself in front of the owner of a small engineering firm, much like the one where I'd worked in Jacksonville. We talked about how I could help them as an organization while moving forward with getting my professional engineering licensure in Michigan. He said he would love to have me come and join him on staff, but he needed at least a two-year commitment to make the investment worthwhile.

It was certainly a fair ask on his part, and weeks of painting and stocking shelves had me interested in pursuing a career. I clearly remember the exact internal conversation happening in my head at that time: "Kerri is exhausted. We have put Laina through the wringer moving her around to seven different homes in four different countries in two years. I'm wounded and exhausted. We tried, we really did, and all we have to show for it is broken health, a broke bank account, and confused isolation. Maybe it is time to say we gave it one hell of a shot, but we came up short for whatever reason, probably something I did. So maybe it's time to give up the grandiose dreams and settle down. We can live normal lives, I can work a normal job, we can build a house here in Michigan near Kerri's parents and raise our kids in the suburbs like sane, normal people." At that moment, it was all there for the taking, all I had to do was give up the vision and give this small business owner a two-year commitment and restart my engineering career. I contemplated it and went home to discuss it with Kerri.

We talked about it for perhaps a day or two, but deep down I knew if I were to cast aside the vision I had been given for making a difference in the world by sharing the Gospel, in order to take this safe, normal path forward, my soul would die. Don't get me wrong, there is nothing wrong with taking a more normative path in life, it is just not what God had prepared for me. I knew it, and more importantly, Kerri knew it. We were both apprehensive about what this meant for our future, so walking away from this opportunity was difficult, but in the end we had no choice. Safety and significance rarely lie down in the same bed. Our decision was made. We would once again choose to take the road less traveled and see where it led. In the interim, I would paint and stock grocery store shelves.

Less than a month following this gut-wrenching decision, opportunity began to come our way. We had an invitation to travel to a very large, ten-thousand-member church in mid-America to interview for a position. The large megachurch was intriguing. The entire time we were there visiting they were all repeatedly asking us to join them by taking this Associate Minister of Missions position. I was certainly open to it, but I will never forget how they totally low-balled us on their salary offer. I literally wrote out a budget for my family of four and plugged in the $26,000 they were offering and asked the guy recruiting me, "Show me how to make this math work." I wasn't trying to be greedy, but I did want to know that I could purchase a simple house and feed my family.

He was a good guy who took this dilemma to their HR Director, who in turn asked him, "Why is this guy asking for more money? Are we in a position where we need to match an existing salary?"

That was the most arrogant, pompous, unspiritual thing I had ever heard from a church! My thoughts were, "No, you are not trying to match a higher salary I had earned elsewhere. My salary last year was $18,000 because I was on the backside of Siberia with my family serving with YOUR international mission board trying to expand the Gospel in faraway places rather than climbing the corporate church ladder. If I would have been here instead, I would have commanded the $40,000 salary that would have to be matched to close the deal. But go ahead and punish me and my family for doing the significant, yet extraordinarily difficult things you proclaim to believe as a ruse to raise all of this money you so greedily parse out to us peons based on our previous year's salary." Is that too harsh? Definitely, but it is exactly how I felt coming home from the mission field to this corporate church mentality.

Because of our children, Kerri was not able to travel with me on my recruitment trip to South Carolina, which started the day after we returned from the Midwest trip. For the South Carolina visit, I was in town for less than two days so I had to make a quick decision, and I did. My first night there I called Kerri and told her we were coming to South Carolina. The next day we closed the deal and I had to rush out to get to the airport. In fact, I had to leave so abruptly that I wasn't even able to view the apartment I leased before I left. The leasing agent asked if I wanted to see it and I told her I didn't have any time and it didn't matter because we had to take it regardless. For Kerri and me, though, it didn't really matter where we were going to live because it was clear that this was our next ministry position. A big part of that was the fact that the people in South Carolina genuinely wanted us to come and they were interested in helping our family transition back to America after the last two years of battle. Curiously, the guy recruiting us to the church in the Midwest called me while I was in Lexington, just two days after leaving his church. He told me he thought the position there was not going to be challenging enough for me. He went on to say he felt that I needed a position where I could lead the ministry myself, rather than working under him or anyone else. Those kind words of wisdom affirmed the decision I had already made. He was genuine in his desire to help me find the right spot and knew my frustration with their HR philosophy, and correctly intuited that I was too much of an idealist to ever hold that frustration internally.

Several weeks later, we landed in Lexington, South Carolina, with two twin beds, two donated chairs, a few nightstands, two beautiful children, and one old Dodge Caravan. I don't remember unloading, but what I do remember is the pastor of Lexington Baptist at the time, Rick Fisher, really wanting to take care of us. They paid us $37,000 as a salary that first year, which was a ton for missionaries who had been earning less than half that amount. He also took us to Scott's Furniture and gave us a $3,500 allowance and told us to get whatever we wanted, as he knew we had nothing. This gift was special to us because when we were leaving seminary we took all the furniture we'd owned and gave it to a refugee family that had come to seminary from overseas and didn't have a single thing. Here I felt we were reaping what we had sown.

Now that we had a bed and some living room furniture, I scraped together $2,900 to buy an old Toyota Corolla at Rawl's Auto Auction with the help of Malcolm Robinson and we were off to the races. In just a few months, a house came available and Rick gave us $3,000 for a down payment. We moved into this house just before Christmas and it would be our home for the next seventeen years. We didn't have nearly enough furniture to fill the house at first, but we didn't care. It was a castle compared to what we were accustomed to during our missionary term and soon people from the church brought us tables, entertainment centers, and Barbie Jeeps for the kids, all the things you need to make it in the suburbs. Don't misunderstand, though, it was still sparse. Our dinner table was an old green card table a family gave to us. It was so ugly Kerri covered it with a light blue plastic tablecloth. The chairs at that table were white plastic lawn chairs. I was oblivious about how embarrassing this had to be for her as a budding homemaker and hostess, but as always she was 100 percent supportive of this extraordinary mission we had embraced, believing there was Divine impact in our future.

With all of these things in place, we began to settle down in Lexington and live a more stable life for the first time since we were in college. Kerri was at home with the girls living out her dream of being a full-time mom and I was working at the church along with spending about a month overseas each year living out my dream of taking the Gospel to faraway places. Lexington Baptist was a very supportive place for our family and we made many dear friends during this time. In ministry, I was able to introduce many of these friends to the significance and sacrifice of world missions through education and short-term trips. It is here that I began to teach and preach for the first time and develop those gifts in my life. It was also here that I began to work out a practical theology of life, sin, and holiness by adding more real life experience to my theological education.

These years were formative for my personal theological journey as I read hundreds of books, took multiple personal retreats to read and write, and had hundreds of hours of conversations. The most memorable of these retreats was to Mepkin Abbey, a Trappist Monastery in Monck's Corner, South Carolina. They would allow us non-monks to come and spend a weekend there on campus for a personal spiritual retreat. It sounded extremely challenging, so I went for a weekend and lived in the monastery, where they live under vows of silence and eat only vegetarian meals.

I very quickly discovered that this was not my ideal environment as one who likes steak and conversation. The retreat, however, was personally enlightening after not saying a word for more than seventy-two hours. As one who is already introspective and highly self-critical, though, I determined I would never do that again. All it really accomplished was it gave me a full seventy-two hours in which to look at all the mistakes I had ever made with no outside voice of reason to remind me of any of the good I had accomplished. Besides the personal introspection, it was interesting to watch the monks who had taken a vow of silence communicate with each other via their own form of sign language with characters written in their palms. As an idealist, I felt this was somewhat self-defeating, but who am I to judge? All I knew was that the life of solitude was not for me and the only vow I took was the vow to never do that again!

Shortly after arriving in Lexington, Kerri and I were excited to find out we were having another child. We were past all the fun of surprises and wanted to know the gender right away; we found out we were having another girl. On August 13, 2001, Kristy Lynne Carnes was born. Chief was actually there for the birth and even stayed with us in the birthing room during Kristy's "coming out party." That probably sounds awkward or strange, but this was soon after my mother's death and we were trying really hard to bring Chief into our family and begin the reconciliation process with him. It was such a joy for him to experience this miracle and he talked about it incessantly from that day forward. People who have never had the honor of witnessing a live birth are missing out on life's greatest miracle. It is a holy and awe-inspiring moment to see air flow into the lungs of this new human, this new eternal soul. Daddy's only previous experience in this realm was waiting in the hallways until I was rolled into the nursery behind a sound-proof glass with "that big-ass shiner." I was really so glad to share this experience with him, my wife once again leveraging personally to bring healing to my broken family.

Kristy Lynne Carnes was named for two people. "Kristy" is the name of one of Kerri's college volleyball teammates at the University of Alabama. Kristy Chastang was a spiritual leader of that Alabama team and her moral convictions and spiritual strength were appealing to Kerri from day one. In fact, she is the reason Kerri chose Alabama over a dozen other schools that recruited her. "Lynne" is Kerri's middle name. After my experience of never knowing where my names came from and assuming they had no real meaning, I wanted all of my children to have names that had real meaning because I wanted to always be able to tell them these stories. I remember that my brother, Hunter, had his first name taken from one of Chief's fraternity brothers. I think his name may have been Hunter Hinkle? I thought it was so cool for Hunter to be named after one of Chief's friends.

We were now a growing family of five and Kerri and I were just sure that on one of my many international trips I was going to be presented with a child who desperately needed a home, so we shut down our procreation process at this point, fully expecting to adopt a fourth child in the near future. Unfortunately, that opportunity never presented itself. Having missed out on that opportunity, we did make space to welcome several exchange students from Central Asia into our home, most of whom we still communicate with today. One in particular, Mirgul Karimova, has become our "adopted" daughter for sure and is certainly an eternal part of our family whom we love dearly and see often now that she has immigrated and lives in Washington, DC.

It was during our first year living in Lexington when I received the call that Mother had died. I think Chief called and told me, but honestly I don't even remember. What I do remember is that I didn't cry. All my tears had been shed already. They were shed in that McDonald's parking lot in Jacksonville, where I threw up from crying. They were shed on that trailer floor in Youngsville, North Carolina, where my heart broke into a million pieces. They were shed on our front porch in the mill village as mother relayed to me her painful past. They were shed in the car I drove away from the nursing home that last time before leaving for Russia as I cried all the way home. They had all been spilled already and to be honest, I was relieved. I was relieved that finally, after at least forty years of suffering, she would find peace. I never had a doubt about her salvation. The last ten years with her had been so extremely sad and heart-wrenching, but now it was finally over. She had escaped from this hellish place and entered into an eternal kingdom where there are no more tears and no more suffering, and I was so happy for her.

I returned to Gadsden to speak at Mother's funeral, interestingly enough, alongside Brother Welch. As I spoke about her, I reminded everyone that every single time I had ever prayed with her in my life, she would bow down low and start out by saying something like, "Lord Jesus, I need you, I know I am a sinner and I need you to save me, Jesus please help me and save me." Not once or twice, but every single time we prayed. It often bothered me that she was never able to fully understand the Gospel and rest in the fact that Jesus had indeed saved her because of her faith and humble confession from the very first time she professed it. She had never really been taught by someone who could show her how to rest in Jesus's mercy and salvation as something he had done for her once and for all and would never take away. All she had ever known was a steady diet of the health and wealth nonsense from the local Pentecostal Church. Even so, Jesus loves a humble confession so much more than an astute theology, so her humble prayers were a source of great memories and calming confidence as we said our final goodbye there in Gadsden.

Individuals have certainly lived harder and more tragic lives than Mother, but her life seems so insanely unjust, especially given the fact that she was such a loving and compassionate person by nature. Yet that is how it generally happens in this world. All too often the strong dominate, demean, and exploit the weak and do so with impunity. This fact is a shameful indictment of the strong, for only a small minority of the strong actively perpetrate these crimes against the weak. These are the really evil people whose destruction is sure. The remainder of the strong, generally a clear majority, all too often sit back and passively allow these injustices to happen, either through personal apathy or a desire to protect their own stuff. Sadly, that was the tragic story of Mother's entire life, as she seemed to always be in the crosshairs of the strong, who brought to her much suffering, while no one came to her rescue until Hunter and I reached adulthood. All is not lost, however, because Jesus promised that many who are first in this life shall be last in His eternal kingdom, while many who are last on this earth shall be first. Shirley Carnes suffered unrelenting and untold injustice in this world, but she will be at the top of her class in that heavenly kingdom. Indeed, she already is, enjoying her reward along with Lazarus and so many others who had a very difficult time in this life, but are having a wonderful time in the next.

Several years after mother's death, another life altering took place. My brother, Hunter, came to faith and radically changed his life after being hostile to the faith for quite some time. Once his children began to grow up, he would occasionally attend church with his wife out of sheer duty. Through this process, he was at least warming up to the faith, though he is a stubborn one and was struggling with his own demons and addictions at this point in life. His oldest daughter made a decision to get baptized at about eight years of age, and I remember him telling me about it with some level of excitement. I wanted to ask him, "Why in the world are you excited over your daughter being baptized into a 'bunch of old wives' tales that don't really have significance for the world today'?" I wanted to challenge him with his own prior beliefs from not too many years earlier, when he'd told me I should not drag my family off to Russia for my own selfish ambitions. I am glad I kept my mouth shut at that time, but inconsistency in rationale drives me crazy. After she was baptized, Hunter's heart began to loosen even more until one day it finally happened: He was sitting on his front porch contemplating the meaning of life and what the future held for him and his family and the future seemed dark and dull. Soon thereafter, he walked into a break room at work and randomly heard a televangelist type say, "And what are you doing for your family? Are you leading your family or not? If not, why not?" These were the words that broke him in an instant and caused him to finally bow his knee to Almighty God.

In 1998 there had been some other words, words which had caused him to stiffen his back and curse God, so there was much to overcome. He had stopped by to visit Mother and walked into her tiny room in the nursing home. As he entered, she looked right at him and asked, "Who are you?" He told me later that was the day he said very firmly to God, "Screw you! Whoever you are and whatever you want, screw you!" Mother's pain and the incredible injustices of her life were too much for him to bear without taking a swing at somebody. God was the obvious choice.

Now, many years later, God had reached out and thrown a counterpunch of His own, which caught Hunter flat-footed by clearly revealing to him the shortcomings of his own life on this earth. Miraculously, Hunter humbly responded. His wife called me and told me, "Hunter has rededicated his life." But I was skeptical. We talked soon thereafter and I told him, "If you have really rededicated your life, get publicly baptized as a sign to all and let's follow Jesus together." I didn't think he would do it and was holding back all of the hope and excitement I wanted to express until I heard him answer this question. He didn't even hesitate. "I'll do it right away," he said. I drove home alone to see his baptism at Southside Baptist Church and remember it well to this day. It was a miracle after all he had been through up to that point and it changed the trajectory of our entire family.

Now, in 2007, five years after Mother's passing, there were only three of us Carnes left and two of us were in the faith. Going home was no longer going to be a demeaning, isolating experience. It was going to be a joyful one as we were now a majority in the Carnes' house. I was so excited about the fact that God had saved Hunter, and saved him long after I'd mostly lost hope and rarely prayed for him after more than a decade of fervent prayer. As a result, I wanted to do something, anything, to show God my gratitude. How, exactly, do you show God gratitude when He does something so miraculous like reaching out and snatching your own brother out of unbelief, anger, and addiction at forty years of age? The only thing I could think of was to give an additional "thank offering" to God as they did in the Old Testament. At that time, they sacrificed animals and produce, which were precious and necessary for survival. I didn't have those, but I did have a bank account, albeit a very small one, so I pulled out my checkbook and wrote a $400 check to a dear friend of mine who was pastoring a very small country church. I primarily wanted to thank God and I did that by giving an offering to one of his very best servants who was laboring faithfully in anonymity. That was a ton of money for me and Kerri at that time, but giving a sacrificial thank offering was a great experience I will never forget. Soon after this, Hunter and Kelli came to visit us and I led them in a renewal of their wedding vows in a small chapel now that they were both believers and the vows carried even more weight. If you are laboring in prayer for a loved one, never give in and never give up! A single day after decades can change everything in an instant.

In my third year of ministry at Lexington Baptist, I became increasingly restless about my next steps. I was reading voraciously and teaching in Sunday School–type scenarios regularly. My teaching gift was developing and so was my appetite to find something challenging and significant I could pursue, as I felt my time at Lexington Baptist was coming to an end. I thought for sure another door of opportunity was going to open up for us overseas, but I was mistaken. This left me living in spiritual tension throughout 2004 and 2005. I remember asking every older Christian leader I could the following question: "If you feel like you have a vision in your heart and you have a great desire to pursue it, should you wait on God to give you a Divine invitation into that vision by suddenly opening a door of opportunity, or should you cast caution to the wind and run after it zealously by faith? In other words, will God always provide a clear open door or is it often up to us to cut a hole in the wall and make the doorway?"

Looking back, it was really interesting to watch godly leaders dance around this question and rarely provide a clear answer. I honestly don't know why, but they all became somewhat political and played both sides. If any of them had been very resolute on one side or the other, I would have probably taken that as instruction and embraced it. As it were, I was kind of paralyzed myself, not having the internal "go ahead" to aggressively seek out my next steps yet feeling I was passively missing those next steps. Thus, by default, I was left waiting.

At this point in our lives, faith steps were not altogether foreign. We had experienced one back in Jacksonville, Florida, when we'd exercised faith into the second missionary journey to Russia and beyond that to Southeastern Seminary. We had also exercised faith in our return to Russia for the third and final missionary journey after losing Jason in Columbia. We exercised faith in moving to Sibye to establish new work. We exercised faith in returning to Russia and not taking a medical leave when our bodies were broken down. We exercised faith when we turned down a secure engineering job in Michigan and I kept on painting and stocking, waiting on God to open a door for ministry. Now here we were, several years into our ministry at Lexington Baptist, and my soul was churning, desirous to exercise faith once again and see what God might do through us next. The vision I had at that time was to start something new overseas, a Central Asian missionary sending agency based in Kazakhstan. The burning question was whether I should courageously resign and go make it happen by faith, or prayerfully wait for a Divine invitation into that work? For that question, I had found no answer even though I had asked everyone from the founder of Youth with a Mission, Lorin Cunningham, to noted pastor and author, Stuart Briscoe. I was, however, about to get my answer loud and clear after years of praying, fasting, writing, and waiting.

It was October 2004, four years into my ministry at Lexington Baptist and the month of our annual global impact conference for missions. For at least two years, I had been thinking and writing about how to best mobilize the international church for missions. I had seen and experienced the results of missionary mobilization as a part of the American church, which had sent hundreds of thousands of missionaries around the world over the last two centuries. What I wanted to see now was the Russian church mobilized for missions, the Ukrainian church, the Kazakh church, etc. I had studied and read volume upon volume and utilized this knowledge to write a full-length prospectus about the subject. In it I explained why this should be our focus going forward and how we, as American missionaries, could get it done. With this in hand, I had prayed and I had fasted. I fasted for an entire week around that time, begging God to reveal to me His purposes for my life and to very clearly open a door for me and Kerri to exercise faith once again, not feeling as though I was living up to my potential.

As the conference approached, I sent my prospectus to the lead Southern Baptist missionary in Kazakhstan. I had known

John from my time in Russia and really trusted him and sought his advice. On the very first day of the conference, he came into my office and told me he had read the prospectus and thought it was brilliant. What he said next was the Divine invitation I had sought so desperately for years.

"Todd, we have to do this in Kazakhstan and I want you to come and do it. You speak Russian, you know the land, you are perfectly set up to do it. If you will agree to come, I will make this position the number one priority on my request sheet and we will get you there quickly based on your previous service with the International Mission Board."

Boom! It was clear. I had written the vision and here was the Southern Baptist missionary leader of the entire country of Kazakhstan saying "I have read your prospectus and I want you to come and fulfill it with me, and I will help you in every way possible." I am normally more analytical when it comes to these types of decisions, but in this instance I immediately answered that I would start packing my bags and we would come as soon as possible. After two years of prayer and long fasts, this invitation was all I needed. We were going back to Central Asia, and soon!

What about Kerri, you ask? I was certainly going to consult with her, but I knew she would trust me on this and would be on board one hundred percent. She had seen me labor over this with prayer and fasting and sleepless nights; she'd seen my struggle and read my proposal. And she wanted to return to missionary work as much as I did, as she was never short on courage. She would certainly recognize this now as the hand of God.

As I arrived home very late that night, Kerri was waiting up to tell me about a dream she'd had the previous night. In her dream, we were back overseas in Central Asia. It had been such a vivid dream for her that she'd gotten the girls up and ready early that morning and brought them down to my office at church to tell me about it, as she just knew it was from God and wanted to tell me that I had to talk to John while he was here. When she walked up to my office to tell me this rather strange story, she looked through the small glass pane in my door and saw me talking with . . . John. She instantly knew in her spirit this was in alignment with her dream and we would be moving to Kazakhstan.

When I finally returned home to explain to her all that had happened that day, she basically beat me to the punch and told me what she had seen. Though she had not heard anything from me about it, she knew what had happened. This has happened more than once in our marriage—situations where Kerri has had a dream or an intuition that was revealed as true within hours. Thus, there was nothing for us to discuss about this decision. It had already been made. All we had to discuss was how in the world to tell our church, our parents, and our children. The next day, I told John we would see him in about six months, and we started laying out plans for our departure to Kazakhstan for a four-year term.

Within the next few weeks, we shared this story with our families and with our church. Our kids were still very young so only Laina could process what this might mean, though she had no real memories of Russia by this time. Kerri and I, on the other hand, had plenty of memories from Russia. This meant that we did not have rose-colored expectations about what lay in store for us with three small children in Kazakhstan. Even so, we had written the vision and now God had invited us to exercise faith to fulfill it. It was exciting even though we knew there was a significant price to pay. As we were making preparations, we decided to take a scouting trip to our future home together, the capital city of Almaty, Kazakhstan. I had been there several times in my annual travels overseas, but Kerri had never visited the country. Before entering with our family, we needed to look at schools and housing in order to have a smooth transition. We were on a fast track with the mission board and I had even figured out how to get my injectable biologic arthritis medicine delivered internationally to Turkey and onward into Kazakhstan, a significant logistical hurdle since it had to be refrigerated throughout the journey.

With tickets in hand and visa applications submitted, I couldn't wait to take on these new faith steps. Then I received the call that would stop everything dead in its tracks. It was a call from the Kazakh Embassy in Washington. The man asked me about my time in Russia in the late 1990s and why I'd left. I explained that our term of service there ended and we returned home. Not the full truth, but not a lie either. He then said words in broken English I will never forget.

"I cannot give you the visa, sir, you are on the list. Do you know why you are on the list?"

"What list?" I replied.

"The *Do Not Enter* list, sir. How did you get on this list?"

"There was a big misunderstanding at that time and they said things about us that were not true. Besides, that was Russia and you are Kazakhstan."

"I wish that I could help you, Sir, but there is nothing I can do. We now have a shared list and if you are on it, you cannot enter either country at all. Perhaps you can call the Russian Embassy and see if they will remove you from the list? As for now, I am sorry, sir. The visa has been denied."

It was so interesting because he was actually trying to help me, and embassy workers never leverage to help anyone. But here he was trying to help, asking about my history and wondering out loud if there was anything that could be done, though no amount of help could get me off of the list. When it was over, I hung up the phone stunned in disbelief. I knew this was a possibility since we had been falsely labeled as spies in Russia and summarily tossed out of the country, but I never thought Kazakhstan would share a Do Not Enter list with Russia. *"How can this be, God? What about Kerri's dream? What about John's invitation to come to Kazakhstan after all the prayer and fasting? What about the years of preparation and the fact that my Russian is still sharp, making me field ready from day one? What about my deep connections in the American church that could be such a support?"* GONE! All of it evaporated in a five-minute conversation about some cursed list somewhere, probably written on old Russian notebooks. I was livid, and I was powerless. The vision for international missions died for me suddenly and violently on that day. I should have buried it and moved on, but I am stubborn and never give up that easily.

With Kazakhstan closed, I decided that I could just go to Moldova and base out of there instead, as I had many contacts in Moldova, both national and international. Kerri and I exchanged our airline tickets and traveled to Moldova in order to scout it out as a possible landing spot from which to fulfill the vision of a Central Asian missionary sending agency. We spent five days there with my good friends Vitaly, Emma, Ivan Ivanovich, Fyoder, and others. By day three it was clear this was not the place for us. They would have all been glad to make room for us there, but it was also clear they didn't need us. The Moldovan church was much more mature than the Kazakh church at that time and I was not interested in having someone make room for me. If I was going to load my family up and move overseas again at great personal cost and sacrifice, it was going to be to a place that desperately needed what I had to offer, not a place that could "find a way to utilize me." Furthermore, I could never do it just because it was something *I* wanted to do; I could only ask my family to sacrifice if I knew it was something *God* wanted us to do. Moldova didn't need me and therefore, I didn't need to move to Moldova. I sent the prospectus to John and told him I would help in any way I could from here in America. Then I buried the idea of ever going back overseas to live. The door had been permanently closed.

I'd thought God had opened the door for us again, so I ran toward it full steam, but it had been slammed shut at the last moment! Looking back, I am somewhat glad it happened the way it did because I am such an idealist at heart, and I had to know for myself that I would return overseas if that is what God wanted for me. Only an experience like this allowed me to test my heart to see if I would really answer the overseas call. God rang the bell and I answered, as did Kerri, so we knew we were willing to return overseas being well aware of the cost of living overseas. With that door now closed in spite of me trying to ram it open, I could be at peace with knowing I would serve the rest of my ministry years here in the US.

Following this crazy series of events, Rick Fisher gave me more responsibility within the church and allowed me to teach a little more, as that gift was continuing to develop. We even began to discuss planting (i.e. launching) a church out of Lexington Baptist that I could lead. Rick knew I needed a new challenge and he was trying to facilitate it in whatever way he could. He and I had a good relationship and my responsibilities continued to grow, putting me in a very comfortable spot. Comfort, however, is not something I have ever found comforting. Quite frankly, I wish I would have been a little better at enjoying comfort in life, but I have always positioned it at odds with significance and therefore it usually causes me more consternation than enjoyment. I do not think this philosophy of life is exactly accurate, or even recommended. It is just how I am built, or perhaps it is my calling. I am honestly not sure which one it is, though I wish I would have provided my family with more enjoyable comfort through the years.

Within months, I began to prepare mentally to pursue a church plant, with Lexington Baptist Church as a sponsor, at some point in the future. I was eager to teach and preach. Just as this idea was gaining some traction, Rick suddenly announced he was stepping down as pastor and moving upstate to pursue a different type of role. This caught everyone by surprise, myself included. I distinctly remember him taking me to lunch just before he went public and telling me in somewhat cryptic language, "You need to decide what you want to do, because people are going to be asking you." He never said it clearly, but he insinuated that I needed to decide if pastoring this church was something I wanted. As he left, he asked the deacons to allow me to preach for the first six Sundays after his departure so that I, as an insider, could help the congregation transition through this emotional process. Looking back, I think he wanted to give me a view from behind the pulpit to see if this was really what I wanted.

My very first sermon after his departure was based on two photos. One was a photo of a raggedy old sailing vessel which was all shot up and barely afloat. I explained that too many people thought this was the state of Lexington Baptist Church just because Rick had taken another assignment. Then I put up a picture of a modern-day destroyer battleship, saying, "In reality, this is the state of the church now that Rick has left, as the church is never dependent on any one man." I certainly honored Rick and his long service at the church and all he had helped us accomplish, but I also rebuked anyone who thought that we were somehow wounded just because our leader had been called to another outpost. We needed to understand that we, collectively, were THE CHURCH, and as long as Jesus is alive, we are a destroyer, not a rickety old sailboat. I really set it up so that it would be somewhat shameful to walk around pessimistic about our future. Amazingly, it worked. We honored Rick and his wife, Debbie, while embracing the fact that we were the church. As such, if we would only exercise faith, we would certainly press on to new heights based on the firm foundation already in place. It was a great compliment for me when Debbie Fisher reached out to me just a few days after that sermon and thanked me for preaching the way I did. She felt honored and was glad to see the church challenged to move forward.

I preached for the next five Sundays as planned and then was told I needed to step back from preaching on Sundays because the congregation was beginning to follow my leadership. The church lay leadership teams felt as though they needed to take their time in going through an in-depth process of a year or more to find the next pastor, removed from all emotion. I took on a lot of additional pastoral duties during that next year and grew quite a bit in my leadership ability as a result. Over a year later, a new pastor was brought in from North Carolina to lead the congregation. During our first meeting, I relayed to him that I had really enjoyed my time here, but I would begin looking for my next position now that he had arrived and wouldn't be here long-term, as I wanted to be fair to him while he made plans for his future staff.

I don't remember the exact time frame, but I think I resigned four or five months after his arrival. My departure was mostly amicable, with only a few notable exceptions of members who took issue with me personally or my decision. Looking back, I was not in agreement with the process that led to the result, but I also realize that the result was God's will and it certainly turned out to be the best result for both myself and Lexington Baptist. The things I wanted to accomplish as a church leader could not have been accomplished within the structure of a very large, traditional church. As it was put to me, I was a known quantity, and as such, I had already made some friends and had some opposition. An outsider, on the other hand, has a "honeymoon period" as a new leader wherein they have the appearance of perfection because they haven't been forced to make any difficult decisions that bring opposition to their leadership, and hence they have additional latitude in the first six to nine months in which to make critical decisions for the church's collective future. Now, as a fifty-year-old leader, I know that to be true, not only in the church, but in business, politics, athletics, and commerce. I am not sure it is the best leadership paradigm, but it is the predominant one and it often works out best for everyone in the end, as it did in this instance because God had just the right place of service chosen for me already and it is not one I would have chosen without walking through these events.

Lena Petrova (Laina Carnes namesake) being baptized in a Russian Lake

Me and Kerri on our scouting trip to Moldova with Fyodor

CHAPTER 16
NEW WINE, OLD WINESKINS

A s I made plans for my departure from Lexington Baptist, I developed a friendship with a local church planter, John Reeves. We began to spend more and more time together talking about church planting options, as he had already planted six churches. His latest church plant was in Lexington—Radius Church. It met at a local elementary school. I really didn't have any desire to join an existing church plant, but my friendship with John was growing. What I wanted to do was to plant a church on my own and shape it from day one. Now keep in mind, I had no idea how to do this at the time, but this was my goal.

As I was preparing for this, John and I were talking one day and he said something very similar to the following: "Hey, man, you have a lot of capital in Lexington and I really think you could make a great impact for Jesus here. So when you leave Lexington

Baptist, why don't you just come to Radius and hang out with us for a while. Then, when you get ready to step out and plant a new church in Lexington, we will send some of our folks with you and help you as much as we can financially. Our folks really get the idea of multiplication and we will have several families that will want to go with you because they really have a heart to reach Lexington."

At this time, Radius Church had fewer than a hundred regular attenders and a budget of less than $100,000, most of which was consumed by existing staff members, including John, himself. I'll never forget him making that unselfish statement. There was no hint of the normal "I am going to protect what is mine." It was 100 percent focused on "Let's make disciples in this town at all costs and I will give whatever I have to those who can make that happen because it doesn't have to be me or mine." I had never seen such openhanded faith in the American church and it was both startling and incredibly compelling. On that very day, I bought what John was selling and determined I would join Radius Church and hitch my wagon to theirs in some form or fashion. Now I just had to figure out how that was going to look for me and my family.

In my last few weeks at Lexington Baptist, I was living in that gut-wrenching faith exercise where you feel called to something very specific, but have no idea how to make it work. Furthermore, you are acutely aware that you are putting your family at great risk in making this faith step so you worry incessantly about being the man Jesus used as an illustration, the one who started to build a tower but ran out of money before he finished and was summarily ridiculed by all for not counting the cost before he started the project. These kinds of faith steps look so brilliant and God-ordained in hindsight when they work out, but make no mistake, they are painful in the moment because there is no guarantee of success and much fear of failure. This instance was no different. I distinctly remember being asked by a local pastor the following question immediately after my resignation: "Todd, how are you going to provide for your family if you step out to plant this church?" Honestly, I didn't have a good answer. As a matter of fact, here is an entry from my journal at the time.

I just had the pastor of a small church plant in Lexington, called Radius, ask me to meet with his elders about possibly taking over there and moving that church plant forward, which might be a good fit. I will meet with them on Friday of this week and I hope we can line up on things. In the meantime, Todd Baine has graciously offered us the use of his second home, rent free, while we plant this new church, which could be a huge blessing and move us forward. That is $1,000/month right there in savings. I am currently raising support as well. I have two sponsor churches thus far and I am working to get others on board. So there are a lot of possibilities for us in this endeavor. These are great steps of faith. In thirty days we will have absolutely no income and only about $10,000 in savings upon which to live, and that will last us only two months as I will have to start paying our insurance payments of about $800/month. So there are obstacles for sure, but we pray that both Kerri and I can find part-time jobs where we can work and make our living as much as possible unless God provides sponsors who will support our family for twelve to eighteen months while we launch. Anyway, that is the latest, we must keep believing and moving forward and reforming the church at large and we are committed to that. . . . God have mercy on me, *a great sinner, but one who is eager to take some risks for the Kingdom of God.*

I was ready and willing to go to work as a bi-vocational church planter for a season and had even begun to pursue positions. I was hoping my engineering background would help me find something and came very close to taking a position in construction management. I knew I needed something that would allow me enough time to do my primary task of planting a church while providing enough income for my family to stay afloat. I was also aware if this professional job didn't pull through for me, I might be pressed back into the painting or stocking or other entry level work to try and make ends meet for a season, although there is no way I could feed a family of five from that type of work. In short, it was nerve-wracking for me as the provider for my family.

If there had been another path forward, I would have taken it, but there was no other way to fulfill the vision I had been given. In the end, Kerri and I counted the cost and made the jump with no promise of a parachute. The one thing I was sure of at that time was the fact that I wanted to plant a radically different kind of church. I told Kerri and others that if I was unsuccessful in planting this new type of church, I was ready to walk away from church leadership and go back to engineering. If this happened, I was going to settle down, make a living as an engineer, and ride off into the sunset quietly. I had no interest in making a living from church payrolls if I didn't firmly believe in their vision and philosophy now that I had a vision of how that should look. Therefore, I had to make this final attempt. We jumped! It was May 2008.

Kerri loaded the girls into the car and went to Michigan for a visit the day following my final day at Lexington Baptist. I was staying at home to look for work, raise support, and start this process. On the very first day she was gone, she called home crying to let me know that she had not been selected for the job at Lake Murray Elementary, the school our daughters attended. This was upsetting because that most likely meant her only job opportunity was going to be ten miles away, across the dam in the Chapin area. That would mean leaving at 6:30 a.m. every morning and returning at 4:00 p.m., which would rob her of being home and available for our children just before they left for school and right when they returned home; she had been able to stay at home with our children up until this point in our marriage. Only as a result of this new faith step was she taking on this responsibility of going back to work.

With this devastating news about the location of her job and all that was going to cost her, I found myself home alone with anxiety beginning to pulse throughout my entire body. Negative feelings and doubts began to ravage me. I had just walked away from a very stable position that paid a really nice salary with benefits and had almost no risk. The new pastor had told me I could help frame my own job description as he arrived, and Kerri could remain at home and not have any of this stress placed upon her. What was I, crazy? Selfish? Foolhardy? All of the above?

After hearing Kerri's tears, I put down my laptop and came out of my recliner so I could lie face down on the floor of our den. It was midday. I began to pray; I began to beg. Just weeks before, I was formulating this church planting plan full of faith and confidence. Now that I had "gone ashore" and burned all the ships behind me, all of that confidence was gone in an instant as my wife's pain increased, leaving my body paralyzed. I lay there for hours feeling alone, anxious, and discouraged. I loved my family and wondered why I would put them at this kind of risk once again. We had somehow survived Sibye and our reentry to America, why did I have to do it again? I wanted a good life for my daughters and wondered how terribly this might end for all of us. As for Kerri and me, what if we were wrong and we were going to be humiliated in front of the thousands to whom we had expressed our plans, perhaps not accurately counting the cost of this faith step? To say it was terrifying would be a grave understatement.

Later that evening, as I sat there alone in my home, I received a phone call from Hill of the Lord Church, a small church plant in Columbia that was receiving any financial support that might come for us. Jessica was on the other end. She was their financial controller as well as a friend I had met on a small group mission trip to India several years prior. Her first words to me were, "Are you sitting down? Because I want to help you believe for something." I had spoken at their church just a few weeks back and had talked about how it is important to continually exercise our faith by always believing for something that is well beyond our reach. If we ever stop doing this, our faith muscles grow weak and we are unable to believe for greater things. My faith muscles certainly felt weak. She then said, "Today I received an envelope with two checks, each for $27,000. Looks like you made budget this year!"

I started laughing uncontrollably. These funds had come from a brother and sister in our community, both of whom knew me well. He had found out about our situation from a support letter we had sent to a church in upstate of South Carolina, a church his daughter attended. His daughter had obviously provided him with the information. Their family had sold a business recently and had some margin to be generous. In the support letter, I had laid out a very minimalist budget showing that I needed $54,000 to keep my family of five afloat for one year while I planted this new church. I was earning significantly more than that before resigning from Lexington Baptist, but was only asking for the minimum since I was planning to work another job as well. With these checks and $8,000 graciously provided by Lexington Baptist members at our going away party, year one had suddenly and miraculously been paid in full on the very day I lay on the floor full of doubt and anxiety, praying and begging for mercy.

As dark as that day was for me, the light at the end of it was a thousand times brighter. God was very clearly saying, "I have called you to the vision and I will fulfill it." I phoned Kerri immediately because I was so eager to take the burden from her and let her know she would not be driving back and forth to Chapin every day and missing out on her primary calling to our children. We rejoiced together as the pressure we had both felt was removed in an instant.

I wish I could articulate what exactly had happened as I saw my faith deteriorate into doubt and anxiety when I heard the pain in my wife's voice and felt my heart sink as the leader of my family. Yet it is not something that can be explained if you haven't experienced it personally. Nor can you explain the sheer joy of watching God provide in miraculous ways when no one else can solve the problem other than Him. With this blessing, we could now go forward in faith and fulfill the vision, though one final faith step remained. You can read it direct from my journal below.

Well after receiving this support I still had to decide what to do with a job offer from Mickey and her construction management firm. She was ready to make me an offer and graciously help me re-enter the workforce, but I called her the day before the offer was due and told her to not even tell me about it. I didn't want to know anything about it because it would just make it harder for me to walk by faith. I told her the only reason I was still entertaining the offer was because I was wondering if God would still be God in nine months when I ran out of the money He had already provided. It was a lack of faith, a "plan B" for me, so I could get back into the development industry and have a fallback plan. So I never even saw the offer and walked, which is totally what God wanted because just a few months later he connected us with Radius in a full-time way and we are now going full-steam ahead with them. They can provide me with a small salary to begin with and we can work toward a normal salary in the future. But I didn't know any of this at the time I had to walk away from Mickey's offer. Anyway, God has been good. . . . Now I am overwhelmed and asking God, "What is it that you would have us do in this community and in our world to go forward?" We cannot "underwhelm" our people with a small vision, it has to be massive! In the midst of all of this Kerri is substitute teaching and I am working full-time at Radius. The break with Lexington seems to have gone as well as possible. Thank you, Lord, for our new venue of service.

That first summer at Radius, John invited me to preach for the first time. They were working through the Ten Commandments throughout the summer and he asked which one I wanted. Instantly, I chose adultery. I had grown up seeing the horrific effects of it, so I hated it with a passion. "It will be easy to preach passionately on this one," I thought. Whenever I had spoken at my former church, I was always in a suit and in a very formal setting on a high stage speaking to five hundred people in each of two services. This day, I was in jeans and an untucked shirt standing on the floor of a lunchroom speaking to fewer than a hundred. I used the illustration of adultery being like the dreaded Guinea worm of Africa. The Guinea worm slips into humans stealthily through contaminated water. Once inside, it starts to grow, preparing to ravage the body while showing no symptoms of its presence. Once it is fully grown inside of the body, it will suddenly and violently burst out of a leg, usually at the shin, a heinous site for all to see. There is blood and puss that oozes out along with this living worm hanging its head out of your shin and bouncing around. Once it bursts out, you have to begin pulling it out slowly, inch by inch, for days or even weeks to fully get it out of your body. If you just break its head off, the rest of the body will decay and bring infection, often killing the victim. So when the Guinea worm is ingested, it is hidden and no one knows. When it breaks out of the body in a bloody, horrifying mess, it is very public and everyone knows.

Adultery is the same way. It starts very small and hidden from the public's eye, but it ends with gross repercussions and public shame and exposure. This sermon, along with this illustration, is still remembered and talked about by dozens of people from Radius more than a decade later. It was the right word at the right time. God had put Radius and my family together in a unique way that day, though none of us knew exactly what that meant just yet.

After this sermon, I went home and was lying on my bed exhausted. At that very moment, Kerri brought the old-timey cordless telephone to me on my bed. It was a call from a gentleman at another local church. Someone had passed my resume to them at least nine months earlier. I had forgotten all about it since I had never heard anything from them. On this particular day, however, after my first sermon at Radius as a guest preacher, I received this call. The nice gentleman explained that they had received my resume, along with hundreds of others, and had narrowed their field of candidates down to three. I was one of the three. I will never forget what he said next.

"So what do you think about that, young man?" presumably expecting me to say that is great and such an honor, etc.

I thought for only a split second and replied, "I really appreciate the call, but I am not interested in your position at this time so that will get you down to only two." I wanted to say so much more, considering they'd had my resume for nine months and never even reached out for a phone call confirming they'd received it. That made it pretty presumptuous to reach out now and expect me to still be available and ready to move forward. How thinking people wind up running churches like this I will never know. I know they don't run their businesses like this or they wouldn't be in business. This was a large church with lots of resources and surely brought with it a six-figure salary, but I had no interest in any of that. I had just stood and preached a powerful message to one hundred people in an elementary school lunchroom, and I would have never been able to preach that type of raw, direct message in this type of church. My gift for teaching about real life issues in common language had been unleashed and I could never go back to formal scenarios where I had to be careful about what I said or how I said it.

My family lived off of the funds we had raised plus income Kerri was earning as a substitute teacher for the next six months. Then, in January 2009, Radius provided us with a salary of $42,000, which we could supplement with the support that had been given. This got us all the way through 2009. John Reeves and I had co-pastored throughout the fall of 2008 and he was now moving to Texas for a position there. I was given the leadership role and we set about the task of making disciples, tackling the tough questions of culture and teaching extravagant generosity to our church. I linked arms with a group of guys within Radius that would become lifelong friends, and we began to reach more and more people with our message. Over the next seven years, we went from one hundred attendees to more than one thousand spread over two campuses. Along the way, Radius members were inspired to begin several impactful nonprofit ministries. Among them were Ezekiel Ministries and Crossover Ministries, both of which are active to this very day.

During this season, one of the most gratifying things I was able to do each year was to write a personal letter to the gentleman and his sister who provided us with that $54,000 gift to get started. Initially it was, "I want you guys to know that the $54,000 you invested in us produced $100,000 that was given to the poor and missionaries from Radius Church this past year." The last letter I sent to them in 2019 said, "This last year the $54,000 you invested in us back in 2008 produced $750,000 that was given to the poor and to missionaries this past year from Radius Church." They'd believed in us and supported the leap of faith that Kerri and I had embraced at very great risk for our family. Out of that combination, well over $4 million dollars have been given to the poor and missionaries by Radius Church since 2008 and thousands of people have been reached with the Gospel.

If you are a person that has either earned or inherited millions of dollars, may I ask what you are doing with it? I am sure you are investing in land, businesses, the stock market, trust funds, etc., all of which is both wise and prudent. But are you investing in the next generation of leaders who can multiply your eternal investment in like manner? I am not talking about $5,000 investments, either. I am talking about six-figure investments! Why are you not finding these leaders and giving them a small portion of the financial margin God has provided for you so they can be free to drive sustainable, godly change in your community and other communities around the world? Why not find five of these leaders and believe in all five? How else can you invest your financial windfalls? If only one of them produces in the same way as Radius you will experience a hundredfold return on your investment in things eternal. Where is this kind of thinking in our world? These strategies are often used in the stock market when investors bet on ten startups, knowing only one has to hit in order to produce a hundredfold return. Why not invest in these more significant goals in like manner? Who is casting this kind of eternal vision to the rich and shouting louder than those peddling common toys? This is the role of the church, to provide a compelling vision to those with resources to fulfill it.

Once during my time at Radius, I went to a very successful entrepreneur and asked him for $10,000 to help a family adopt a child. $10,000 was a rather small sum to him at that time and he gladly provided it. With his help, the family was able to move forward with the adoption, which would have been in jeopardy without the $10,000 gift. Looking back, it was a very simple thing to connect this giver with this wonderful opportunity and I only wish I would have done so more often, as it is so gratifying to see faithful givers align with eternal initiatives. To this very day that generous gift continues to bless everyone involved and it brings me great joy as I watch this child grow in a nurturing home.

Our family when we first went to serve at Radius Church, which was meeting at Midway Elementary School

Teaching at Radius after we bought our first building in downtown Lexington, SC

CHAPTER 17

FAITH STEPS

A s strange as it may sound, I have a love/hate relationship with leaps of faith. Without them, life can seem boring and insignificant. With them, life can be very exciting, but also anxious and unnerving. My journey has been a journey of faith steps, generally taken every four to six years. After seven years as Lead Pastor of Radius Church, I felt a clear pull back into the marketplace, so I made another leap by stepping down at our peak. I knew it was time for me to take on the next challenge and I have always said that pastors and football coaches almost always stay too long and destroy their own legacy. I didn't want to make that mistake. Upon leaving, I was able to transition into a role where I invested five years working as an executive at a fast-growing small business in our town, SouthernMED Pediatrics. After five fast and furious years in that role, that season came to an end and I branched out to start a new real estate brokerage with my friend, Todd Lyle, which we appropriately named Todd Realty Partners. In the not-too-distant past, I honestly thought my faith steps might be coming to an end as I entered my fiftieth year. Thankfully, and frighteningly, they are not. And once again, God confirmed it for me in His supernatural way.

I was feeling especially low one day after having some diffi-cult things happen within my family. That Sunday, I went to work out to try and exercise my way out of the doldrums. Afterward, I decided to return the call of a woman I had never met but who had called me on the previous Friday to tell me that she had been given my name by God while she was praying for political leaders, and that she was specifically praying for me and my family. She had said in her voicemail that she was an older woman, and she sounded very kind and didn't ask for anything in return. She said I could call her if I wanted, but if not she just wanted me to know that me and my family had been prayed over for the last several weeks. I had no idea what "given my name by God" meant and after twenty years in ministry, I can be somewhere between skep-tical and cynical about things of this nature from strangers. When I called her I went right to the point and asked her exactly where she got my name, assuming it was from some type of published prayer list of elected officials from all over the nation or similar. She replied by telling me that my name had been given to her by God, not by man.

This made me even more skeptical, as I have seen and heard it all with people over-spiritualizing things as a faux spiritual power grab. I relayed to her my skepticism and she wasn't offended by it at all. Then, the more we talked, the more I realized that she didn't have any hidden agenda and was really sincere and humble, very rare characteristics. After about twenty minutes, I thanked her for praying for my family and told her that I really hadn't wanted to call her back, but felt compelled because she specifically said she was praying for my family. As we were about to hang up, she asked if she and her husband could pray for me and I agreed. They started out by praying the armor of God over me from Ephesians and then they spoke a specific word of knowledge over me just as my calculus teacher had done thirty years earlier. Without going into all the details, she painted a picture of the future as it could be by faith, with spiritual battles yet to be fought and victories yet to be won. As we hung up, I was in tears and told her how I hoped she was right in what she prayed, wanting to believe it was true, but unsure of it still. As of now, I still don't know all that this meant or where it will lead, but it was clearly a Divine word of encouragement to prepare me for the next assignment, which I am now earnestly seeking. It is just a reminder that God is merciful to us in both the good times and the bad.

Looking back over the first half of my life, it is clear to me that I have lived a different kind of existence. Because of my idealistic personality in combination with childhood wounds and insecurities, I would be the first to say that my journey has not been what I would label as a joyful one. Don't misunderstand; I have been given some great gifts and had great moments of joy. The gift that is my wife, the birth of my three precious children, the miracles provided in times of faith, and the sacrificial support of dear friends in times of trouble have been so much more than I deserved and have certainly brought seasons of joy. Yet these times of joy have often been surrounded by anxiety, insecurity, self-doubt, shame, and general self-loathing. Having never lived in the skin of another, I have no firm concept of how much others experience these types of negative emotions, but I feel as though I have experienced more than my fair share based on what I have seen and experienced as a pastor, privy to the private lives of so many.

In looking for causality of these types of negative feelings, I have never had a desire to assign blame, as they are probably more my fault than anyone else's. Looking back, however, there are discernible patterns for these kinds of dispositions. For example, I never went hungry as a child, but there were times when I worried about it with good reason. I also never went without life's necessities, but I remember at least one summer when Mama White had to sew clothes for us. Memories of scarcity such as these have caused me to feel as though I was running from poverty all my life. It doesn't matter if I make $50,000 or $150,000, I always feel that sense of scarcity, as though poverty is always nipping at my heels and will overtake me any minute. Others I know never appear to experience these types of negative feelings and I can't help but think they were cemented during my childhood years of insecurity.

In addition to financial insecurities, there are also personal insecurities that have to constantly be beaten down. Knowing what I know about so many others after a lifetime of ministry, it is really difficult for me to use the term *abuse* when talking about my childhood. *Abuse* is a very strong term that I only feel comfortable attributing to the most devastating of circumstances, of which there are many. On the other hand, people who come from healthy family environments, such as my wife, are always appalled at the things we experienced in my home. I have always downplayed it and dismissed it as "not that bad," but the deep-seated impacts of our nuclear families are real for all of us, whether good or bad. I really don't enjoy contemplating how it might have skewed my perceptions of reality, but I find myself doing just that more and more as I get older. What I have come to understand is the reason I have always refused to even contemplate it is because it somehow feels weak, like I am searching for some type of crutch or excuse in life. I don't ever want to put myself in the realm of victimhood in that way, as that in itself in paralyzing. But by the same token, I don't want to pretend that the impacts of my particular roots are negligible. I want to acknowledge them here in the last half of my life so that my transparency might serve as a type of encouragement and guide to the millions of others who have walked a similar path. My hope is that they won't wait until fifty years of age to assess their own situation honestly, allowing them to work through it in their early years rather than working around it for the first half of their lives.

As I have done that very thing over the last several years, it has brought to me several great insights into who I am and what I might accomplish in my last few years on this earth. For example, I am often told that I have great empathy for others, though that is hard for me to believe. If this is true, it is because I have loved so many family members and church members who have suffered so greatly and learned empathy as a part of that very painful process. I am told I am too aggressive in some of my stances in society when it comes to issues of justice and the relationship of the strong and the weak. There is no doubt this is true and has its genesis in a lifetime of seeing the strong dominate the weak with impunity in my own home and elsewhere, with long and disastrous results for all parties. I am often told I am a restless soul who has great courage to try new things. In reality, I am an insecure soul who has an internal voice always telling me I am not good enough to do (fill in the blank). Every time this happens, I take a good, long look at whatever it is I'm feeling not good enough for, whatever it is that my internal voice says is way above my pay grade. When I define what it is exactly, I am so driven to destroy this negative voice in my head that I feel as though I now must attempt that very thing, if for no other reason than to make the negative voice shut up and stop accusing me of being a failure.

Thus, I make the attempts not purely out of courage, but more often out of fear that the voice inside of me might be right! When the internal accusing voice says you can never do something, it always follows that with, "You are not nearly what everyone thinks you are and you will eventually be exposed as a failure." Strangely enough, after having done everything from business to politics, from church planting to missionary work, I have discovered that no amount of accomplishment will squelch the internal accusations and self-doubt. Perhaps it was planted there during the trauma of my childhood? Perhaps it is just my natural disposition? Nature or nurture, I do not know, but I assume I will be buried with it. It will not, however, travel with me beyond the grave. It is part of the old man, not part of the new man that God is renews day by day. It has certainly had a negative impact in my life at times, never allowing me to simply relax and enjoy successes and the simple joys of life in the same way others have enjoyed them. I lament that fact, but it was seemingly unavoidable. On the positive side, however, it has driven me to do things I could have never accomplished without its constant slander and accusations, so there is some good with the bad.

If you understand what I am talking about here, you understand how this internal battle can be hell on earth. The battle rages between the ears and easily costs so many of us much joy and rest during our sojourn. The price can be high, but there is an opposite side to this coin as well. The opposite side is the fact that this very clear and constant view of my personal shortcomings has caused me to abandon all hope of being approved or accepted by

God on the basis of who I am or things I have accomplished. As it is stated in the Bible, I put absolutely no confidence in the flesh. I am painfully aware of how even my best deeds are like filthy rags in God's sight, and I am not sure how many others see that clearly into their own hearts. When you can't see this undeniable reality within yourself, you are susceptible to having an inflated view of your standing before God and others, which is dangerous. My introspective bent, along with this clear view of self, always errs on the side of a deflated view of self, for better or for worse.

For example, when I fasted for a week I grumbled much of the time, hoping God would hear and answer but often not really believing anything would come of it. When I moved to the very ends of the earth, I did so seeking to bring the Gospel to people who desperately needed it, but I now know it was also to win the admiration of my missionary colleagues and others. When I left the security of a large church to start a new church, I was filled with just as much fear as faith. Every time I have attempted or accomplished something, I am acutely aware of how I am a mixture of both good and evil, with most of my attention focused on the evil within rather than the good. After two decades of ministry, I have seen many others who are peripherally aware that they are a mixture of good and evil, but they are somehow able to focus primarily on the good inside of themselves, while only glancing at the evil. In truth, I envy these people. They certainly live more joyful lives because of this perspective. My wounds, however, prevent me from living life in that lane. These same wounds also have an upside. They are what has driven me to speak forcefully against oppression, empathetically to those who are mourning, and humbly to those who are suffering. I do not want any more wounds in this life. I honestly don't think I can handle many more significant ones, as I have only divulged a few of them here in these pages and not even the most painful ones. But without these scars, I am sure that I would not have a story worth writing.

As we approach the conclusion of this story, I would like to finish where we started by sharing with you those last few hours Chief had on this earth at the house where it all started, 3704 Roselawn Drive. Before I do, however, I want you to understand how my story ended with Chief. After coming to faith at twenty-one, I was angry with him for at least a decade. As I met people who were raised in more nurturing homes, I began to realize just how abnormal my home was as a child. I honestly didn't consider my home to be that bad as a child because I had numerous friends whose homes were significantly worse than mine. So it wasn't until I was exposed to homes that were healthy that I realized how far from healthy we really were. This awakening, along with watching Mother's painful mental and emotional demise during this season, caused me to be very angry with Chief. Often, we verbally sparred about the past and his treatment of Mother. Interestingly, I never took any issue with his treatment of me and Hunter, it was always his treatment of Mother. Going back to my initial assessment, I think this is because of the shame I felt and continue to feel for not being able to protect her from him. There is no shame in being dominated by your father as a young boy, but it has always felt shameful to me that I couldn't rescue Mother from that domination. This shame leads to deep-seated anger, which takes time to work through and diffuse. For me, it took almost a decade.

After sparring with Chief all through my twenties, Mother died when I was thirty-one-years-old. From that point forward, I began the reconciliation process with Chief. First of all, I opened myself up to understand more of his background and just how harsh his life had been as a child and as a young man. I began to understand how he had been blindly lured into his own father's footsteps of adultery and addiction, never intending to bring that kind of pain and turmoil in our lives. Second, I matured as a person.

Forgiveness is a hard thing to give when you are somewhere between immature and arrogant. As I matured and entered my thirties, I was able to clearly see all of the good that Daddy provided for me instead of solely focusing on the bad that happened to Mother. I think the bane of all twenty-something's existence is the harsh judgment we so often place upon our parents during this decade of transition. As a twenty-something, you are now an adult and as such, you feel fully entitled to objectively judge your parents' actions during your first two decades of life. Unfortunately, you often do not have children yourself, or if you do they are very young. This means you are now speaking authoritatively about things you have never experienced and know precious little about, namely, raising children. That was certainly my story. In my twenties, I had no clue about the pressures Chief faced day in and day out. I had no clue about the responsibility that was on his shoulders and the demands on his life. I am sure he felt the incredible weight of pulling us all up out of the poverty of the mill village. I also didn't know just how harsh his childhood had been at that point, yet I was ready to hold him to a level of perfection that was neither fair nor helpful.

Finally, and perhaps most importantly, I realized he was my father and I loved him deeply, warts and all. As a more mature person in my thirties and eventually in my forties, I was able to embrace the fact that Chief was far from perfect, but I didn't really care about that anymore. I was at a place in life where I could literally see his painful regret upon his face as he grew older, along with seeing my own parental failures multiply with more responsibility. Now, as my forgiveness process progressed, I lost all desire to chastise him for the things he had done wrong. Rather, I only wanted to remind him of the things he did right. As a father myself, I quickly realized that is what I was going to want from my children because I was doing plenty of things poorly as well. Life is like that. We are all flawed, simple people trying to do the best we can for the next generation but doing it a lot more poorly than we envisioned when we started.

Throughout my twenties, I wanted to take Chief to task for all of his misdeeds. When Chief would talk about making "mistakes," I would reply, "Those weren't mistakes, those were intentional choices. There is a big difference!" In my thirties, I moved beyond the anger and haughty vengeance. Looking back, I should have gotten there a lot sooner. As a young father myself, I was able to fill my heart with love and forgiveness, no longer harboring a desire to hurt anyone with those old memories, so I buried them deep in the recesses of my soul and refused to think about them. I began to change so that I only wanted to bring joy to Chief's life by inviting him into my family's life and developing a healthy relationship with him. By the grace of God, I was able to accomplish these things before the window of opportunity closed forever, and it was ultimately fulfilling. I have sought both vengeance and forgiveness in my life, and forgiveness is by far the most gratifying.

For the last decade of Chief's life, he became one of my best friends. He was homebound more often than not so I called him most every day just to talk whenever I was driving. We would rejoice over my victories and he would coach me up on my failures. We enjoyed talking to each other as friends during this season of life because the reality is we are very similar. I enjoyed sharing my victories with him because he sacrificed so much to prepare me for those victories by making me work as a child and educating me as a young adult. Fathers are unique in that way. In every victory you experience in life, you can openly share every detail with them without feeling as though you are boasting because both of you are fully aware that your victory belongs to your father just as much as it belongs to you. That means the two of you are like teammates, able to celebrate all of your wins together in the locker room of life. I had to do most of this by phone from South Carolina to Chief back home in Alabama, but I took my family there as often as possible because I loved bringing joy into his life by sharing my family with him. Every time we visited, all five of us had to pile into one small bedroom with three of us on a bed and two on the floor. This was the very same bedroom Kerri and I shared for a summer when we went home to help Mother. I never cared about that, though, because I wanted to be home and honor my father in his old age while helping him heal from the wounds and regret of his past. I wanted him to be free from the guilt and shame of it all and that process was part of my healing as well. I think I was successful in that endeavor. I sure hope so.

As I was finishing this book and searching for old photos, I found a card I had sent to Chief for Father's Day at some point in the past. I have no idea when I sent it, but based on the looks of the card, I think I sent it around 2010. I actually found this card while cleaning out Chief's belongings in our house after his death in 2017. This card was one of the few things I had written to him that he actually kept. That fact alone made me smile when I found it because the message it contains is the exact message I wanted to dominate his thoughts in his old age. Honestly, I am more proud of writing this Father's Day card than I am of writing this entire book! I am sure that I tried to communicate these thoughts to Chief in various ways to assure him that he was forgiven and had my blessing, but I am so glad, even relieved, that I took the time to write them out so clearly on this particular Father's Day. Here are the words from the card, a card I want placed in my casket when I die because I feel like it is me at my very best:

Chief,

Just wanted to write you a note of thanks as my dad. As I think back about my first twenty or so years, I thank you for taking me bird hunting a lot, for flat bottom boat fishing trips, for teaching me to gold and helping me in baseball. I thank you for making me work in the summer and teaching me a good work ethic. I appreciate you working me hard when I was hungover to teach me the law of cause and effect! Thanks for the trip to Lake Guntersville to hit balls and play nine holes. Thanks for your extravagant generosity with me when I was in college, paying for everything and allowing me to graduate debt free and with a car. I took that for granted at the time. Thanks for helping me out with wisdom and support in my lowest point in life, my being booked into jail after my accident and Jason's death. If not for you at those times I might have quit, but you supported me even in my rebellion. You taught me a lot Chief and your footprint is large in my life and family today. Being a dad is VERY HARD. *I now know that, so thanks for all the joy and wisdom you gave to me. Love, Todd*

As one who has already made the journey, let me encourage you with the following: if there is anyone in your life that desperately needs your forgiveness and your blessing, write it out to them today. It is the greatest gift you will ever give to anyone and it can be given whether they "deserve it" or not. One day you will be so proud of providing them with this blessing. Forgiveness is that way. It is very difficult to provide it when you feel as though you don't need it yourself. However, when you start to realize just how much you desperately need it yourself, it suddenly becomes much easier to provide it to others. Act today, you may not have tomorrow.

Chief holding Kristy the day she was born after witnessing the birth himself

The Carnes men in Chief's last year of life, always representing with our BAMA gear

CHAPTER 18

THE GOOD CONFESSION

With Chief still in his hospice bed, we managed to get through Sunday night with regular doses of morphine and other prescription medicines to keep him somewhat calm. Then, late Monday afternoon, it happened. I was seated at the back of the den looking through my iPhone when suddenly he called out my name for the first time since I had arrived the day before. "Todd, Todd, where are you? Todd, come here."

I went to him and held his hand through the arm rails of the hospice bed. He looked at me and then he looked up with tears in his eyes and said, "Todd, I am asking Jesus to forgive me of my sins, I'm asking Jesus to save me, son. Jesus, save me and take me to heaven."

Daddy didn't cry, and he didn't pray either, at least not in my lifetime. But right here, literally on his deathbed, he cried and he prayed. More importantly, he asked *me* to come to him and join as a witness. I told him I loved him and that God loved to save great sinners like me and him, so he was in good hands and good company. I assured him that God saves us when we cry out for mercy and He does so not because He has to, but because He wants to. That was the full extent of our conversation. He was holding my hand and he looked up again, staring into the ceiling for a few minutes before dosing off back to sleep. I was stunned, as were Brenda and Janice. No one knew quite what to say or do in that moment. If I had not seen it myself, I would have never believed it. Seriously, I would have taken no one's word for it, for I was even second-guessing my own experience because it was so surreal. If another would have recounted it to me, I would have said they manipulated him somehow and put words in his mouth while he was sick. I would have found a way to question and discount the entire experience. But I saw it with my own eyes and heard it with my own ears. Twenty-five years of prayers answered at last.

I thank God that I saw it with my own two eyes. It was unsolicited. It was pure and it was clear. It was humble and it was supernatural because he had no way of knowing I was even in the house as I sat on the couch behind him not saying a word. Yet at that very moment he called out to me! It was me that he wanted at his bedside as a witness. The black-eyed infant. The Asshole. The cocky, drunken teenager. The beloved engineer. The foolish missionary. The family preacher. It was me that he wanted to come near while he called out to Jesus for salvation, the only One who can save sinners and deliver them into a Heavenly Kingdom. It was me who heard this good confession with my own ears and struggled to recount it even to my own brother because it seemed so utterly unbelievable. It was unexplainable that this was the first time he had recognized me since my arrival the previous day. It was as if he had a small window of lucidity and when it came, he wanted to make peace with God and he wanted me to be a part of it. Surely he knew I had prayed for this for twenty-five solid years, as evidenced by the written reminder I have carried in my wallet that entire time. I saw it. I wept.

Thirty-six hours later, Chief died. It was 4:18 a.m. on May 31, 2016, and I was right beside him. I was holding his hand and telling him that I loved him, telling him that I was proud of him as my father, telling him that he was a good daddy for me and Hunter, telling him it was okay for him to go now and we would be coming right behind him. It was a holy moment, as I was able, along with my brother and his wife, to usher Daddy out of this life and into eternity. For anyone who just saw the ending of this story, it might seem like a great ending to a nice story about a quaint little family living in a small, blue-collar mill town in Alabama. In reality, it was a truly miraculous ending to a very complicated tragedy that unfolded over five decades at 3704 Roselawn Drive. And, for me, it was the beginning of the freedom to look back, uncap, and share this story of acceptance, grace, and redemption.

Chief as I remember him

The hospice bed where Chief died in our house at 3704 Roselawn Drive

BURYING HOME

As one who has served as a pastor for more than twenty years, I have walked families through a lot of funerals. One thing I have always noted is when a person had to bury their second parent, this event would often have a much greater impact upon them than the death of their first. I was forty-seven when Chief died and, as usual, experience brought to me the insight I couldn't understand previously.

As a child, I was always very close to my mother. When she died twenty years ago, her death was difficult, but she had fallen victim to early onset Alzheimer's and died not even knowing who I was after three long years in a nursing home. Thus, in some ways, her death was more of a relief, an end to her decades of suffering. Chief died at the age of eighty. His body was severely run down and his suffering was great those last few years, so there was some relief in seeing his suffering end as I held his hand and watched him breath his last at 4:18 a.m. on May 31, 2016.

The very moment he was gone, a new reality suddenly hit me and it hit violently. I was immediately aware that I was not only going to bury my father, I was going to bury "home." When my mother died there was definitely a void in life, but home remained. Daddy was there, my neighbors were there, my house was there. With my father's death, I was struck with the painful reality that "home" had to be buried as well. Strangely enough, home seemed to be the hardest funeral of them all because there is no relief in losing home. Home was not suffering, home was not in pain and home was not lonely, so there is no relief in this burial of home. It was a funeral filled only with loneliness, accompanied by the uneasy feeling of being unhinged in this world, tossed out to sea with no more anchors. This was not true, of course, but it was the overwhelming feeling and one that can easily overwhelm us.

In my case, my father still lived in the house where I grew up, which made it even more difficult. As I walk through our old house, there is a memory in every corner. There is the back of the den where I paced and cried as a child with an infinite number of ear infections. There is the front of the den where I dutifully sat in front of the television serving as my father's human remote control before the electronic versions existed. Further back in the house are the doors I painted for the first time as I learned how to paint, and the bathroom where I fought acne as an insecure teen. Perhaps most special to me is our modest 6' x 6' concrete porch with indoor/outdoor carpet where I sat on the steps so many after-noons—talking to a girlfriend on a cordless phone, waiting to be picked up by friends, having meaningful conversations with my mom, or just taking a break after hosing off all the filth that was a part of working a full day as a laborer for Carnes Construction Company.

Now all these things are going to be lost. They will be sold off to someone who doesn't know about them or appreciate their history. Things that are sacred for me will become common for them. As for me, I can never go home again. I will have the memories, but "home" is no more. I can never see those things again and have those memories flood through my mind. What's worse, I know this will cause the memories to fade even faster. Over the last twenty-five years, I have lived in fifteen different homes within Russia, Thailand, Cyprus, and five different states within the United States, yet no matter how far or for how long I journeyed, I could always go home. It was an anchor for me. I had a root in that mill village that was twenty-five-feet deep. That root anchored me to something, to certain people that seemed almost eternal in a world where everything else is constantly shifting. Now suddenly, almost violently, that root has been yanked from the ground and laid on top of the soil to dry out and die in just a few days. I'll be the first to admit I was not prepared for this. I was prepared for my father's death, as he had been diagnosed with lung cancer six months earlier. I was not prepared to lose this anchor. I was not prepared for my brother to put his arm around me and say, "Now we are orphans." I was not prepared to bury home.

Before leaving home after Daddy's funeral, I loaded up my wife and daughters and drove them through the mill village where my grandparents worked and where my parents grew up. I showed them the simple mill houses and explained to them what life was like for my parents. It was a life without cars, without travel, and with very little money as the children of Dwight Manufacturing Cotton Mill workers (aka "lintheads"). It was a life where an old spare tire was my father's most treasured toy, a life where meat was a luxury to be enjoyed only on Saturdays when a chicken was butchered. I wanted them to see and understand just a small portion of the deep roots I have in this area and take some pride in their strong, humble roots on Sandusky Lane. I don't know if they "got it" or not. But it was goodbye for me—a painful goodbye that reminded me how even the deepest roots in this world are temporary. A goodbye that reminded me of why God says we are to live as aliens and strangers in a foreign land, just passing through on our way to an eternal home, a home that does not even have the words *goodbye* or *death* in its vocabulary. A goodbye that shatters any and all silly notions about experiencing "heaven on earth" and replaces them with a simple "earthly longing for heaven."

Rest in peace, Mother, your suffering has ceased. Rest in peace, Daddy, your deathbed confession saved you. And rest in peace Mill Village Home. The roots you provided for me have helped me weather all the storms life has delivered thus far, and they will see me through to the very end!

Revelation 17:16–20

"I, Jesus, have sent my angel to give you this testimony for the churches. I am the Root and the Offspring of David, and the bright Morning Star." The Spirit and the bride say, "Come!" And let the one who hears say, "Come!" Let the one who is thirsty come; and let the one who wishes to take the free gift of the water of life come. . . . He who testifies to these things says, "Yes, I am coming soon."

Amen. Come, Lord Jesus.

SPEAKER INFORMATION

Would you like to invite Todd Carnes to speak at your next event? With experience as a pastor, business owner, and elected official, he has experience speaking to businesses, churches, civic gatherings, and elected officials.

To make a request or to connect with him personally, please visit

www.buryinghome.com

Made in the USA
Las Vegas, NV
03 March 2021

18885076R00164